Black Suicide

HERBERT HENDIN

Allen Lane The Penguin Press

First published in
the United States of America in 1969
by Basic Books, Inc., New York

First published in Great Britain in 1970 by
Allen Lane The Penguin Press
Vigo Street, London W1

SBN 7139 0138 1

Printed in Great Britain by
Lowe & Brydone (Printers) Ltd, London

TO Jo

Acknowledgments

I WOULD like first to acknowledge my debt to two teachers who, although playing no direct role in this study, nevertheless contributed to its taking place. Professor Otto Klineberg, whose study of the effect of environment on Negro intelligence remains a classic in social psychology, influenced me, while I was a student of his at Columbia College, to go on to study psychoanalysis. During my psychoanalytic training I was fortunate enough to be able to study with Dr. Abram Kardiner, the pioneer in the application of psychoanalysis to social research. Kardiner and Ovesey's book, *The Mark of Oppression,* remains the major psychoanalytic contribution to the study of the Negro problem in this country.

Anyone undertaking today a psychoanalytic study of any aspect of the Negro problem is indebted to a number of outstanding psychologists and sociologists who have established a solid body of knowledge on which current work tries to build. Although I discuss in detail only work that is immediately relevant to the current subject matter, I would like to acknowledge my debt to those whose thinking has particularly influenced or stimulated my own: Kenneth Clark, John Dollard, E. Franklin Frazier, Gunnar Myrdal, and Thomas Pettigrew.

I am grateful for the help of many people and organizations who contributed directly to this study and would like to thank in particular those indicated below:

Dr. Elizabeth Davis, Director of the Psychiatric Division of Harlem Hospital, made it possible to see patients at Harlem Hospital and gave me the benefit of her advice and cooperation during the entire project. Dr. Austin Moore and Dr. Hugh Butts, both of Harlem Hospital, helped keep me informed of suicidal admissions to the hospital.

Dr. Morris Herman, Professor of Psychiatry at the New York University College of Medicine, and Dr. Arthur Zitrin, then Director of Bellevue Psychiatric Hospital, made it possible to see patients at Bellevue Hospital.

Dr. John Cotton, Director of the Psychiatric Service of St. Luke's Hospital, and Dr. David MacDonald, Chief of the Psychiatric Clinic at St. Luke's Hospital, made it possible for me to see patients at that hospital.

Psychologists who assisted in the testing of patients include Milton Klein, R. A. Ferdinand, S. David Greenbaum, and Martin Diner. Dr. Arthur C. Carr not only tested some of the subjects himself and did the analysis of the test results but gave unstintingly of his time and energy in helping to edit the manuscript.

Mr. Louis Weiner, Acting Director of the Bureau of Records and Statistics of the New York City Department of Health, and Mrs. Freda Nelson, Principal Statistician of the Bureau of Records and Statistics, helped me with statistical problems in connection with this study. Miss Patricia Cubbison, formerly a statistician in the Bureau, did most of the actual tabulations and preparation of the graphs.

Dr. B. Ruth Easser of the Columbia University Psychoanalytic Clinic read the manuscript and made valuable suggestions concerning the presentation of the material, suggestions that have been incorporated into the final text.

Professor John Nelson of Columbia University and Dr. Hugh Butts of Harlem Hospital and the Columbia University Psychoanalytic Clinic read the manuscript and made helpful suggestions for its improvement.

The Center for the Study of Suicide Prevention of the National Institute of Mental Health awarded me a grant (MH 14633-01) that helped me to complete this project.

My wife, Jo Hendin, spent many months helping to write, rewrite, and edit the entire manuscript. Her invaluable assistance was exceeded only by her love and encouragement, which made the writing and rewriting a source of pleasure.

H. H.

New York
July, 1969

Contents

1. *The Problem* 3

2. *Suicide and Violence* 9

3. *Suicide and Male Homosexuality* 49

4. *The Older Men* 72

5. *Women and Suicide* 93

6. *Three Suicidal Adolescents* 122

7. *Conclusion* 132

APPENDIX I. *Figures and Graphs* 148

APPENDIX II. *Psychological Testing by Arthur C. Carr* 156

INDEX 169

Black Suicide

1

The Problem

MOST people, both white and black, are surprised to learn that among young urban Negroes suicide is a serious problem or that in New York, for example, suicide is twice as frequent among Negro men between twenty and thirty-five as it is among white men of the same age. The high frequency of suicide among older whites has led to the misconception that suicide is a "white" problem, obscuring the fact that among young adults of both sexes, particularly in urban areas, it is actually more of a black problem.

If the suicide of young blacks has been obscured or ignored, the high frequency of homicide by Negroes has not been similarly neglected. Not generally realized, however, is that black homicide reaches its peak at the same twenty-to-thirty-five age period as black suicide. Of what significance are these facts? Is there a relationship between black suicide and black homicide? Do the statistical differences between Negro and white suggest more profound psychological differences?

An understanding of black suicide was made possible by use of psychoanalytic interviewing techniques emphasizing free associations, dreams, and fantasies in order to study intensively twenty-five black patients who made suicide attempts. These suicidal patients do more than tell us about black suicide. They dramatize the general pressures and conflicts of Negro life; they hold an enlarged mirror up to the frustration and anger of the black ghetto. Unfortunately their problems vary only in degree from those of large masses of urban blacks on the bottom of the social scale.

A previous study in Scandinavia* made clear that suicidal patients were an excellent barometer of the pressures felt by everyone in that culture, whether they succumbed to them or not. This was confirmed by observation of non-suicidal patients and non-patients. Suicidal Swedish patients presented an exaggerated picture of the pressures of life in Sweden; the only help they provided in understanding suicidal patients in Norway was by way of contrast. For example, in Sweden there is a "performance" suicide related to the rigid concern with achievement that characterizes the culture, while Norway derives from its puritanical rural areas what can best be described as a "moral" form of suicide that reflects a concern with sin and punishment.

The fact that suicide had varying psychological significance in related but distinctly different cultures led me to write: "The ways to express individual and social maladjustment are clearly limited; suicide, neurosis, crime, alcoholism, and a few others. It is reasonable to assume that these ways vary qualitatively (that is, in meaning and significance) as well as quantitatively, not only from country to country, but also among the subcultures of the United States."† The present study is an

* Herbert Hendin, *Suicide and Scandinavia* (New York: Grune & Stratton, 1964).

† Herbert Hendin, "National Character," *Columbia University Forum*, Winter, 1964.

exploration of this assumption. It deals not merely with differences in frequency but more importantly with differences in the motivation and significance of suicide in black American culture.

While the focus of this study is psychosocial and not statistical, a detailed study of the figures for white and black suicide made with the help of the New York City Bureau of Vital Statistics provided a necessary background for the psychosocial investigation that followed. Inadequate study of national figures indicating an eleven-to-four ratio of white to black suicide has obscured the frequency of suicide among young urban blacks.

The New York suicide rate is much closer to the white rate than the almost three-to-one ratio of the national figures.* More important, a breakdown of the New York City figures reveals the surprising information that, among blacks of both sexes between the ages of twenty and thirty-five, suicide is decidedly more of a problem than it is in the white population of the same age. The graphs in Appendix I showing the New York white and black male suicide rates for the years 1920, 1930, 1940, 1950, and 1960 clearly illustrate this phenomenon. It is only after the age of forty-five that suicide among whites rises to heights so much greater than that of blacks of the same age that it causes the white suicide rate to rise to a total level higher than that for the Negro.

It is worthwhile to contrast the black and white homicide rates in New York for the same census years 1920 through 1960. It will be seen that black homicide reaches a peak during the same age period as black suicide, although at all ages it is significantly higher than the white homicide rate. While it is true that homicide rates refer

* The white suicide rate in New York averages, for the past forty years, about 1.75 times the rate for blacks. For the last census year of 1960 (census years are the years in which such rates can be most accurately calculated), the New York City white rate was 10.8 as compared with a black rate of 7.8—a ratio of only 1.4 to 1.

to victims and not to perpetrators, the overwhelming majority of blacks murdered in New York are killed by other blacks of approximately the same age. The high black suicide and homicide rates in the twenty-to-thirty-five age group cannot be attributed merely to the Negro revolution and the generation influenced by it, since the pattern goes back to at least 1920. An explanation of the relationship between black suicide and black homicide is one of the aims of this study.

Although statistical studies seldom give answers to the most significant questions, they can help to define the problems and even point the direction in which to look for solutions. For example, a startlingly high 50 to 60 per cent of the black suicides in New York each year are by jumping. While jumping as a method of suicide is high in New York for whites as well—between 25 and 30 per cent as compared with 5 per cent in the total population—its surprising frequency among the New York black population warrants some discussion.*

Although a particular method will often be of unique psychological significance for the individual patient, availability and familiarity are major factors in determining the frequency of any method. For example, 15 per cent of suicides in Norway are by drowning, while drowning as a method of suicide has a world-wide fre-

* Since 1958, in line with a revision in statistical procedure, people killed by a fall from a high building are listed by the New York City Department of Vital Statistics as suicides rather than accidents unless there is indication from the Medical Examiner to the contrary. The figures for both white and black suicide by jumping have gone up two-and-one-half times since the revised procedure was adopted. Prior to 1958 there had to be evidence of suicidal intent to list such deaths as suicides. The suspicion arises that the current figures may include people who were pushed from the building and were uninvestigated homicides. It should be kept in mind, however, that the greater incidence of black suicide in the twenty-to-thirty-five age group goes back as far as 1920. Moreover, even in the period prior to the revision, jumping was twice as frequent among black suicides as it was among white suicides.

quency of only 1 to 2 per cent. However, with a fishing, sailing, and shipping tradition that goes back for centuries, the sea for Norwegians plays a central role in conscious and unconscious life, is a major theme literally and symbolically in literature and art, and for most of the people takes on personal and communal significance. Since Norwegians live on the water more than other peoples it is perhaps not surprising that some of them choose to die in the water as well. As life in Norway centers on the sea, so life in Harlem centers on its endless number of five-story tenements. So much of Negro life is lived in and on top of these tenements that they fill the conscious and unconscious life of their inhabitants and come to provide a tragic setting for the case histories that follow. Claude Brown's *Manchild in the Promised Land* perhaps best dramatized for the white community the degree to which sexual experience, fighting, and drug usage takes place on the Harlem rooftops. Jumping from the top floors or roofs of such buildings is possibly the closest that many black people come to a feeling of escaping tenement life.

The wretchedness of ghetto life has been described often enough to need no summary here. Psychodynamic analysis remains, however, the best tool for revealing the human consequences of the ghetto on the majority of its black inhabitants, and for revealing how racial institutions operate to shape and misshape the lives of black people. The cases that follow at first seem to be only individual histories, but gradually patterns emerge, so that by the concluding chapter it is possible to describe the delicate interaction between culture and character that forms the core of this work.

The twenty-five black subjects, thirteen women and twelve men, were admitted to hospitals following suicide attempts. While almost all subjects had inflicted sufficient damage on themselves to require hospitalization, both very serious and some not so serious attempts are included, since experience has shown that both are necessary to give a representative picture of the problem of suicide in any particular culture. These patients were seen as often as necessary to obtain an adequate psychodynamic picture of them. Usually seven or eight visits were sufficient, although in one case fifteen visits proved necessary. A battery of psychological tests was administered to almost all of the subjects. Professor Arthur C. Carr's summary of the test material is included in Appendix II, and his comments on individual cases are recorded as footnotes in connection with those cases.

2

Suicide and Violence

THAT black suicide and violence are related was suggested by the statistical data of the last chapter. In their hovering between depression and rage, the young suicidal blacks who are the subject of this chapter make clear the nature of this relationship.

Peter Churney* is a light-skinned youth who had thought of killing himself since he was twelve. At nineteen, after two previous suicide attempts, he swallowed thirty thorazine tablets after telling his mother he would sleep late in the morning. When she eventually discovered him, he was in a deep coma and was admitted to the hospital.

In discussing the cause of his suicide attempt Peter said angrily and bitterly, "I have my own reasons for wanting to end my life. There's nothing going for me. I get no pleasure from anything. Some people like their family. I don't. I never have. It's not their fault. I grew up

* All the names in this study have been changed.

being only for myself. I've been in real trouble since I saw my father killed."

In describing his father's death in great detail, Peter called him a "nut." He said his father had a good job for a Negro but was convinced people were plotting against him both at work and at home. His suspicions that Peter's mother was having affairs led him to jealous rages. One night when he was beating her in a particularly savage way, the police were called. When they arrived, his father began shooting at them. Peter, who was seven at the time, was trapped in the room with his father, who had five guns and, although wounded, continued to fire until he was killed.

Peter thinks he had been overly sensitive even before his father's death and would not talk for hours if someone hurt his feelings. After the death of his father, he became very belligerent and fought frequently with his teachers. When his ninth-grade teacher said he needed a beating, Peter replied that the teacher needed his throat cut. He waited for the teacher with a knife and hammer but friends discovered him. His grandfather came and beat him, whereupon he stole his grandfather's gun and went looking for the teacher until friends got the gun away from him. Shortly after this incident Peter withdrew from school.

Soon after leaving school he was caught in an attempted burglary and sent to a detention home for five months. He needed money to buy "pot," "dope," and "acid." He says his kicks have lately been ruined and he gets no pleasure from drugs. Three years ago, after his release from the detention home, he began to stay home and watch TV for long periods. He became morbidly suspicious, feeling that his friends were plotting against him. He also became violent at home. One day he wrecked the house and was then hospitalized.

A preoccupation with violence pervades his story. As a young boy he came to admire Hitler's ability to kill millions of people and subsequently thought that he might get kicks from killing. His hero is the executioner in a James Bond film. He says he had the idea of going on a rooftop and shooting people but adds lightly that this was before "that guy in Dallas" did it. Although he feels killing is masculine and sees nothing wrong in it, he now imagines it without pleasure.

He has had thoughts of knifing his mother and brother although he says they do nothing to provoke him, stating that it does not take much to make him want to kill. He makes the point that his murderous fantasies are not accompanied by anger. He was often angered by my questions, saying, "Why should I tell you anything?" or "I don't wish to talk to you." When his anger was pointed out, he would deny it, and try to convince me that if he seemed angry, he was only "acting."*

At this time he is more concerned with suicide than homicide, saying that he is on a suicide course and that nothing can stop him. He believes he has no future. As a boy he wanted to be an archaeologist and now wishes he could make movies like Sergei Eisenstein, whose films *Ivan the Terrible* and *Alexander Nevsky* he has seen six

* Peter's Rorschach test alternates between percepts of hostile content ("mouth of a cannon," "atomic-bomb explosion") and those having a passive feminine implication ("a vase," "flowers"). His initial responses to the Rorschach test were "a mask" and "a helmet" (Card 1), reflecting attempts to protect himself from a world seen as threatening. The percept "wolves with sheeps' heads" appears to reflect a combination of the passive and the aggressive with the further implication of distrust for external appearances.

While the Rorschach and the interviewing made clear this patient's difficulties in controlling his murderous rage, he scored quite low on the Hostility Inventory. This low hostility score was also true of the one other patient (Leroi Nifson, pages 49–54 ff.) who was a potential mass killer. Both boys denied ever feeling anger although their associations, dreams, and Rorschach gave overwhelming evidence to the contrary. The same need for denial and for picturing themselves as "cool" that comes out in their interviews is reflected in their inordinately low Hostility Index scores.

times. He likes movies in which the grotesque becomes beautiful and in this regard has great admiration for actor Jack Palance. He knows he will never get what he wants; at nineteen he can hardly read and cannot write. Yet he is intelligent, informed, and articulate and says he is knowledgeable from watching TV.*

Soon after his present admission Peter began breaking the furniture on the ward and was transferred to a state hospital. In explaining his violent behavior Peter admits that he did not like a doctor who would not let him call his friends for company, but denies that he acted in anger. Bored and restless on the ward, he says he broke the furniture to break the monotony.

He was surprised when I appeared after his transfer to continue our talks. His mood softened somewhat, and till the end of our hour together he put aside his characteristic belligerence and spoke to me in a milder manner.

Peter then revealed that he is homosexual, stating that he has known it with certainty for two and a half years. At thirteen or fourteen years of age, as part of a group, he had one heterosexual experience which he did not enjoy. While he is only attracted to pretty young boys, he has avoided any overt homosexual experience. He does not feel he would get pleasure even from homosexual relations and also denies homosexual dreams or masturbation fantasies. He seems to be trying to check all overt sexual expression, having stopped masturbation at sixteen because "it wasn't right"—most likely because it brought him close to the homosexual expression he tries

* His full-scale IQ on the Wechsler Adult Intelligence Scale (WAIS) was 101—far above average for this group. More strikingly, he knew the answers to such test questions as "Who wrote *Faust?*" "What is the Koran?" and "What is the main theme of the Book of Genesis?" Nevertheless, on the Sentence Completion Test (SCT), he indicated: *When I think back I am ashamed that:* "I did not go to school longer." *I used to feel I was being held back by:* "lack of education." *He felt inferior when:* "competing with other people."

to suppress. If he did engage in homosexual relations he says he would want fellatio performed on him or would want to do the inserting in anal intercourse.

He also began to complain about his mother. He said that she never understood him, that she tried to exert too much control over him when he was a child, and that she was too filled with "rules and regulations." He was somewhat critical of her when he said she "messed around" in recent years with a married man, a former friend of his father.

Peter's twenty-three-year-old brother has a day job in a hospital, goes to college at night, and intends to become a lawyer. He and Peter have never been very close. Peter envies him for his good looks and for his ability to get what he wants.

Peter related a dream that he had the night after his destructive outburst in the hospital:

> He was searching for an orange drink. He could not find a place to get it and when he finally found one he did not have enough money to buy it.

He stated that he often dreams of pursuing a cold drink. He recalled a nightmare from childhood in which he was sitting on a sofa eating an orange, and a black bug was crawling on him.

The need for a cool drink following his destructive behavior on the ward seemed to be an attempt to "cool" his anger and was consistent with his wish to be able to be angry in a coldly detached way. The theme of "pleasure interfered with" that ran through his sessions (drugs that no longer give "kicks," violent fantasies that no longer give satisfaction) appears in both dreams. Since he describes his mother's skin as orange-colored, the orange is a particularly likely symbol for her breast. He is not aware of how much his rage and frustration relate to his need for her. Although emphasizing his hatred of her—she has never understood him, has been closer to his brother, and has "messed around with other men"—he has never tried to live away from home. The bottle of orange soda may be a symbol for the penis, reflecting his hope that he could be nurtured by it as a substitute for his mother's breast. His statement that he would only want fellatio performed on him or that he would do the inserting in anal intercourse seems to be a denial of his passive wishes and is consistent with his desire not to recognize his dependent needs.

The dream in which he is unable to buy the drink reflects his feeling that he lacks what is required to get what he wants. That dream also led him to recall the black-bug nightmare of his childhood. The phallic-shaped black bug is most likely a self-image—one that relates to his seeing himself as detestable because of his violence, his sexual feelings, and his identification through such emotions with his black father. He sees himself literally and figuratively as blacker than he is, as no better than an insect that should be exterminated.

Although Peter rejected the idea that his temper and suspiciousness might suggest that he was following in his father's footsteps, he later admitted that the possibility had occurred to him. He was quite taken aback, however, at the suggestion that his father's death might have been a form of suicide.

One might think that the violent death of Peter's father made his case idiosyncratic. Anyone who has worked or lived in Harlem knows, of course, that experience with violence is common. Violent death had personally and significantly affected the lives of five of the twenty-five subjects of this study. In the case of three of the men, their fathers had been murdered (in one case by a sister of the patient). One woman's husband had been murdered and another woman had grown up without knowing her father, who had been sentenced to life imprisonment for a murder committed at the time of her birth.

Nor was Peter's problem with homosexuality unusual for our male suicidal patients. Although Peter was a non-practicing homosexual, three of the other eleven male patients in this study were actively homosexual. More will be said concerning Negro male homosexuality in conjunction with suicide in the next chapter.

The mixture of despair and violence that characterizes the lives of the black suicidal patients seems even more tragic when seen in the men five to ten years older than Peter, men who have lived long enough to experience more fully the bitterness and disappointment of life in the ghetto. The next two patients have had the frustrations of adult life superimposed on almost non-existent childhoods, yet they are typical representatives of the violent suicidal blacks.

Harrison Eliot is a dark-skinned man of thirty-three, who became acutely depressed and suicidal after being fired for drinking on the job. Drinking and depression, however, have marked his life since his estrangement from his wife and children five years earlier. Although his wife blamed the break-up on his drinking and fighting, he felt their marriage ended because she "fell out of love with me and was unfaithful."

Harrison has a violent temper which he feels might make him kill.* His worst outbreaks have been with po-

* His Thematic Apperception Test (TAT) stories were replete with hostility and killing, either murder or suicide. The "mother-son" card of the TAT (6 BM) was interpreted by him as "A policeman breaking bad news to someone's mother. The son is dead. Killed in gun battle." On the WAIS he functioned at the borderline level of intelligence, with an IQ of 72. His single discrepantly

licemen. For example, a policeman once told him curtly to move on and he objected. The policeman hit him and in the fight that followed he threw two policemen through a window. As a result he spent two months in jail. During a Harlem riot he was carrying a whiskey bottle and mingling with the crowd. He had "come to see what was going on." When a policeman jumped out of a car and broke his bottle with a night stick, he fought and again went to jail for two months. Because of this episode he lost his civil service job as a hospital attendant. He has not worked steadily and is usually fired for drinking.

He has one friend, a married man with nine children, with whom he drinks on weekends. Otherwise he is alone at home watching television. He often buys whiskey with his home relief money and drinks in the hallways of the tenement where he lives, or sits and drinks on a bench thinking about his life. "Once in a blue moon I go to a movie," he says, "or I go to watch a ballgame in the park." He goes to both alone.

His childhood had a similar lonely quality. His father, a railroad chef, was robbed and beaten to death when Harrison was four. His mother, whose strictness and severe beatings he still recalls, died when he was twelve. Harrison was then raised—or rather grew up—with relatives. His brother was in frequent trouble with the police. His sister had a "nervous breakdown" precipitated by having been raped by her older half-brother and becoming pregnant. As a boy Harrison felt inadequate. He was poor in sports, shy with boys and girls, and had little to say to anyone. As a young man he felt inexperienced when he met his wife and married her when she became pregnant.

Two dreams that he had on the night of his admission to the hospital suggest his motivation for suicide:

high score in the WAIS was on picture completion and suggests paranoid features.

He had his civil service job back at the hospital. Helen, an older married woman he met during the last year of his marriage and saw until two years ago, wanted him to go out with her but he turned her down. He was then going out with Helen's friend, Beatrice.

He murdered his former wife and her boyfriend and then killed himself.

He says he often dreams of Helen. He had wanted her to marry him, but she refused and eventually ended their relationship. He had never been interested in Beatrice.

Being fired from his job revives the pain of many other disappointments: with his wife, with Helen, and with the death of his mother. In his dream he tries to reverse what has happened: he has the security of his old job and it is he who is rejecting Helen.

In reality Helen helped to curb his rage. Five years earlier he had bought a gun with the intention of murdering his former wife and her boyfriend. When he told Helen his plans she took the gun away from him. After rejecting her in the dream he acts on his rage toward his wife and her boyfriend although, significantly, he must immediately atone with his own suicide.

Harrison resembles Peter Churney in that he has at times come close to committing murder. His sporadic violence and his drinking seem to be the only remaining ways he has for dealing with the total frustration he feels about his life. His drinking appears to be a self-destructive way of drowning his rage. He mentions that several of his friends drank themselves to death but does not seem to be aware that he is following in their footsteps.

Owen James, a twenty-nine-year-old who could easily be taken for white, turned on the gas in his wife's apartment, put a sheet over his head, and fell asleep with his head over the stove. When his wife came home she found him and called the police.

Claiming he still wants to die, Owen says no one can stop him from killing himself. He says there is "no place in the world for a fellow like me. I'll always be on the same level, I'll get nowheres, I can't read or write."

He has been married for five years and separated from his wife for the past five months. His wife wanted him to leave the house because of his inability to hold a job and his drinking. During his marriage he worked for three years as a dishwasher but he never made enough money. After he began to drink and had trouble holding a job his wife began to run around with other men. While he has hit her often and she has called the police several times because of this, he says he never hurt her. His anger toward her is so great that he has had fantasies of killing her. He says he would never do so, however, because of their two children.

His anger toward his mother borders on fury. He refused to see her in the hospital and flew into a rage when questioned about her. Six weeks before his suicide attempt he drank too much at his mother's house and without provocation assaulted his elderly uncle. His mother gave him fifteen dollars and told him not to come back. He replied that she would not have to be bothered with him any more. Though they have had quarrels like this several times before, he reacted more strongly this time than he had in the past. He took a job at a resort for a month but lost it a few days before his suicide attempt because of his drinking.

Owen's childhood is a story of hunger and rejection. He describes it as "awful," adding that "poor people shouldn't have children." He remembers having to beg for food at the local grocery. At the age of five he was sent by his parents from their home in Virginia to live with an aunt in the North. Soon after, his parents separated and his mother came North for him. He feels he was better off living with his aunt.

His color caused him as much pain as his poverty. Owen's father, though Negro, was lighter than he, while his mother, he says angrily, "was a full-blooded Indian who passed for Negro because she feels if you are Indian you are nothing." Owen was picked on as "white" by Negro boys who told him to "go to a white school" because he did not belong with them. His school career was further marked by his inability to learn to read. Although he saw a school psychologist about his reading, he was unable to improve.

Owen's father did manual work, drank heavily, and had difficulty holding a job. He died when Owen was seventeen, and his mother then married a man twenty years older than she. Owen had no overt difficulties with his stepfather and continued to live at home. Nevertheless his drinking and fighting began around the time of his mother's remarriage, and he was arrested several times for drunken and disorderly behavior.

During this period Owen started going out with women, most of them older than he. Before he met his wife he had made a similar suicide attempt with gas a month after the end of a relationship with a woman twenty years his senior. She wanted to marry him but her son objected. Owen insists his suicide attempt was not related to losing her.

Angered by the implication that he needs his wife or

anyone else, Owen attributes his suicide attempts to the feeling that he is blocked everywhere and has no future since he cannot make a living. He married only because he thought his wife was pregnant. He later found that she was not and he now feels trapped by his marriage. Although he is separated and says he dislikes his wife, he cannot support her and his children and at the same time remarry. He concludes quietly that he will kill himself, stating that being in the hospital is a living death, the same as being dead.

Owen's violence, like that of Peter Churney and Harrison Eliot, seems clearly to originate with feelings of maternal neglect and rejection. Like Peter's and Harrison's, Owen's anger toward his mother is interwoven with his need for her. His first suicide attempt came one month after breaking up with a woman twenty years his senior. His current attempt came one month after the acute break with his mother. It will be seen that with several of the subsequent patients a rupture with their mothers precedes their suicide attempts.

Owen seems similar in several respects to Harrison. Alcohol, loneliness, sporadic violence, and hopelessness mark their lives. An older woman seems to have helped both gratify their frustrated dependency needs and helped them to keep their anger under control. For both patients separation from their wife is crucial. Neither has any inclination to deny or "cool" his anger.* During his first few interviews Owen was quite open in his anger toward me. He said angrily, "I don't wish to talk," and added with

* The violence of both is readily evident in the Hostility Inventory and the Rorschach tests. Owen's views of women are extremely negative; he refers to "whores" on the TAT and says on the SCT that *Most women:* "are bitches" and *I wish that my mother:* "had never gave birth to me." He has a relatively high score on the "assault" category of the Hostility Inventory. While his full-scale IQ is only 82 and many of the tests must be administered orally since he cannot read or write, his vocabulary reflects a much higher potential; e.g., *I was most depressed when:* "I found out that existence was nothing."

fury in his voice, "Why should I spill out my guts to you?" In his last few sessions he became more friendly and cooperative and seemed to be a little more trusting.

Owen had a problem with his racial identity that Harrison did not. He had been persecuted by blacks for being white. He was furious with his mother for denying her Indian identity and passing as a Negro. This may relate to the feeling that he could have passed for white but did not. The one other patient who has been raised as a Negro but whose mother was not Negro will be seen, not surprisingly, to have more than average confusion concerning racial identity.

Owen does not consciously blame being Negro for his feelings of hopelessness. He says he has to tell most people that he is Negro. He focused rather on his deprived childhood and his failure to learn to read and write. He states he has never been happy in his life. He regrets having succumbed to his wife's pressure to marry and feels financially trapped by having to support his children. He sees no future open to him because he can't earn a living—that is, enough money to support a new family as well as his old one. He sees no possibility of any change in his life situation, a feeling that is reflected in his mood of angry desperation.

It is impossible to say whether Owen, Harrison, or Peter is more likely to commit suicide or murder. The violence of all three has its source in maternal frustration. Although Peter lives in a world of homosexual fantasy and tries to escape the pain of his life through drugs, Owen and Harrison were able to marry despite their anger toward their mothers and women in general and have turned to alcohol as a refuge from difficulty. Yet in the degree to which all three are overwhelmed with violent impulses, the extent to which they feel trapped in an unalterable life situation, and their sustained mood of angry desperation, they have a great deal in common.

The rage and violence that mark the lives of the black suicidal men are equally characteristic of the black suicidal women. The next three patients not only demonstrate this, but provide graphic illustrations of the usual origin of this rage in maternal deprivation and cruelty.

Ina Tracy, a tall thirty-one-year-old woman, has made two serious suicide attempts after violent fights with friends. In describing one of the fights she says, "I beat her as long as she moved. As long as she moved I kicked her. Blood both frightens and excites me."

Ina has thought of suicide since her Alabama childhood—itself a history of rejection and violence. She says, "My mother once told me that she wished I have been born dead or that she had gotten rid of me. The way things worked out, I wished it too. She kept telling me that when I was born, everyone was getting rid of babies. She was never happy over anything I did."

Her parents never married or lived together, although Ina's father lived nearby. Although her mother forbade her to see him, she would sneak away to visit him every day because he was nice to her. Her mother criticized her continually by saying that Ina was just like her father.

Ina says of her childhood that there was "not a day without a beating. My mother would make me break a branch and she'd beat me with it—hit me wherever it landed. I wanted to take her and choke her to death. Wished that I would die or she would. She only wanted me to go to school, work, and to go to church." She had nightmares as a child in which someone was about to choke her. These dreams appear to have expressed fears of retaliation for her wish to choke her mother. Although

Ina feared the beatings, she reached the point where she did what she wanted since she was beaten anyway.

Ina was teased in school for being tall but does not feel that she was in many fights during that time. One fight she did recall involved a girl who was chasing her. While she was running from the pursuing girl, she saw her mother, who she knew would be furious at her running away. She turned and fought with the girl and had to be pulled off her.

At seventeen she told her mother she had never liked boys. When her mother replied that she should, she decided to have sexual relations with the first boy who was willing and soon after became pregnant. Her mother put her out of the house but took her back before the baby was born. In the years that have followed she has had infrequent sexual experiences and has never wanted to live with a man. When the baby was two Ina left the child with her mother and at the age of twenty came alone to New York. She has not seen her daughter in five years, but is preoccupied and guilty over this desertion.

While Ina has often since childhood wished she were dead, she made her first suicide attempt at twenty-one, feeling then as now "disgusted with everything." Ina has always feared the dead. She has a recurring nightmare which she remembers specifically having at the time of the suicide attempt that followed the violent fight with her girlfriend. She saw a very large man who had been dead a long time, so long that one could smell him. Her height, her fighting, and her mother's disparaging insistence that she was like her father—all contribute to her masculine self-image. She feels men have an easier time than women since they can fight and protect themselves better. They are also freer to leave rather than be left.

Ina viewed death as a quiescent state, free from violence and loss of control. Living itself was an act of violence in which the only image of peace was a "big dead man."

Although with me she was depressed rather than angry, she alternated closely between suicidal and homicidal fantasies. One night after having been treated for her suicide attempt and discharged, she came to the outpatient department in an agitated state. Because the doctor on duty did not admit her she returned with a gun in order to kill him. But then she decided to go to her therapist, who arranged for her hospitalization.

Ina demonstrates as well as any patient in this study the close conscious relationship between suicidal and homicidal fantasies that was so frequently observed in this group.* Considering the maternal neglect and abuse she has experienced, the origin and extent of her rage are not hard to understand. While she would like to be able to love and care for her child, Ina's own frustrated dependency needs and the rage they engender make this impossible.

During a suicide attempt in which she took sixty aspirin tablets, Agnes Carreth, an attractive twenty-two-year-old woman with bleached red hair, considered killing her husband with a razor while he slept. Her marriage is breaking up and she does not feel she can go on without her husband. He has told her he thinks they should be apart and has been seeing an old girlfriend, Ellen.

Six months ago in a quarrel over her husband's visits

* Ina scored highest of the group on the Hostility Inventory, testifying to the prominence of hostile expression in her life. SCT completions were replete with reference to failure, fear, the wish to die, and anger toward her mother. TAT stories dealt openly with themes of suicide. A tenacity and perseverance in her behavior were inferred that suggested that she might ultimately succeed in killing herself.

to Ellen she hit him and smashed her hand in fury through a window. When she hits her husband she says he restrains her but does not strike back, adding that she does not know what she would do if he did since she has been hit so much all her life. "If my mother hit me now I'd kill her," Agnes said.

Agnes was born in New York the third of four children. After her parents separated when she was four years old she saw her father only once, when she visited him with her mother. During that visit she recalls him holding a knife in his hand but her mother, while confirming the visit, has told her that she does not remember the knife.

Agnes' mother remarried shortly after the breakup of her first marriage, sending her two older children to live with their grandmother. Her mother and stepfather had seven children of their own over the next ten years. Agnes says she had to care for them and received no love from either parent. Her mother and stepfather fought constantly and Agnes would step in to protect her mother. Both parents beat Agnes severely and frequently. She says, "My mother never gave a damn about me. She was loveless. So was my grandmother. My mother didn't even care when my stepfather bothered me." Agnes was then twelve. Agnes went to the police but her mother would not file a complaint. "She always put a man above her children," Agnes says. "If my mother were dying I would be glad and I'd spit on her. I feel the same about my stepfather."

When Agnes was fourteen her mother and stepfather separated. A year later she was taken from her mother because her mother was always out and neglected her children. Agnes was in a children's home for a while and then lived with her grandmother, who made her leave school and go to work after the seventh grade. Of her, Agnes says, "That woman was only interested in money."

When Agnes was seventeen she took her grandmother's advice that she live with her older married sister. Until then she had been too busy fighting with men, competing with them in sports, or being their pal to become sexually involved. When she lived with her sister she began to copy her more feminine ways. She met a man five years older than she and soon became pregnant. Agnes says she did not love him and could not stand his touching her after she became pregnant.

After the birth of her child Agnes went back to her job as a file clerk, while her sister cared for her daughter. Agnes is often impatient with her child and sometimes fears she will grab her and choke her. She has terrible dreams in which something does happen to the girl. Yet when things are going well with her husband, she enjoys her daughter. Agnes mentions times when all three of them play and romp on the floor. Without her husband she feels she will be of no use to her daughter since she will spend her days crying for him.

Agnes feels her inability to have a child with her husband is a major source of her marital difficulties. Her husband wanted her to become pregnant even before they were married and still seems eager to have a child with her.

During her interviews Agnes was free to express both anger and pleasure. Once when she seemed sullen she was asked if she were as angry as she looked. "Angrier," she replied, and went on to say that "if you are mad at one person [her husband] you are mad at the world." She began another interview by complaining that I had come later than I had said I would. She says she gets angry easily and holds a grudge, yet never stays angry with her husband. "He can always make me laugh." She similarly went from anger to laughter during the interviews. She related to me directly and personally. For example, she wondered whether I believed in God, stating she would not marry a man who did not. She once had a boyfriend who did not and she prayed for him, offering to do the same for me if I were a non-believer. Agnes showed in general less emotional constriction than the majority of the patients in this study.

Soon after her admission to the hospital Agnes had the following dream:

> She was with her husband. She and her sister were quarreling. She pushed her sister out of the window. She ran down the street. She told her, "Joan, I'm sorry, I love you." To show how bad she felt, she went up to the window and jumped herself. Nothing happened. She did it again. She received a gash on her face and her husband stopped the bleeding with a scarf. They went to a doctor. A scab had formed. He pulled it off. He put some jelly on her head. It was like water dripping over her mouth. She feared that she couldn't breathe.

Agnes talked of Joan, who was bigger than she. They had frequent fights which Agnes felt she had to win since she was older. Agnes feels her mother always preferred Joan. "She would get more than me." She remembers with particular bitterness a Christmas when Joan received a doll three feet tall and she was given one eight inches tall.

About five months earlier she had a big fight with Joan at a party for her brother Tom, who was going into the service. Joan boasted that she had won and Agnes came back two days later to fight again. She hit her sister with a bottle and went after her with a knife. Eventually others stopped the fight but her sister's husband was slightly cut while taking the knife away from Agnes. Fighting had characterized her life since she went to school. There she was always in trouble for what she describes as "my tomboy ways and my fighting."*

* On the Hostility Inventory she received one of the highest scores in the group, particularly on the "assault" category. In a TAT story dealing with suicide, she depicted death thus: "God is standing here. After death the woman would feel peaceful and have no more worries." In the presence of her poor control, further suicide attempts or assaultive outbursts seemed likely.

Jumping from the window in the dream reminded Agnes of a situation that occurred when she was twelve. She often stole clothes for her doll from local stores. When her mother discovered this she made Agnes undress and then beat her, saying she would beat her again in the evening. When her mother came into the room Agnes was on the window ledge threatening to jump. Her mother pulled her in and beat her anyway.

Agnes is able to see the relation between her violent impulses toward her sister (and husband) and the need to atone for them with her own suicide. This led her to talk of her religious beliefs as a Quaker (Mennonite). She has been praying for her husband to stay with her but feels it has not helped. She gets angry with God sometimes and then asks His forgiveness. She says she may not be meant to live here on Earth, where she is so unhappy, but with God instead.

Agnes felt that I was the doctor who was opening up her wounds, causing water to drip over her mouth. This led her to talk of her fear of water. As a child she had persuaded her grandmother to let her go swimming, claiming she could swim. She jumped in, could not swim, grabbed a ladder, pulled herself out, and threw up. Since then she does not go into water over her head. To this day when she is anxious she has difficulty in catching her breath.

The wounds that are being opened up by her husband and me and that are taking Agnes into "water over her head" are those of her childhood: her mother's rejection of her and preference for her sister. Her impulse to slash her husband's throat with a razor while he slept has its antecedents in her feelings toward her mother and her sister. Her sister also seems a safer target for her rage than her mother or husband.

Ina Tracy's childhood experience with violence came from a brutal and rejecting mother. While Agnes' mother was equally rejecting and also quite violent, Agnes associates violence as much with her father and stepfather as with her mother. Even if her first memory of her father with a knife is not a genuine recollection, it reflects a picture of a violent male that she certainly received from the age of four from her stepfather.

However, Agnes' greatest rage, like Ina's, is reserved for her mother. She becomes furious when she says, "If my mother hit me now I'd kill her" or "If my mother were dying I would be glad and I'd spit on her." Recall Ina's remark about her mother: "I wanted to take her and choke her to death."

Although Agnes resents having been burdened with the care of her siblings while still a girl, there is some evidence that this experience may have been emotionally beneficial. Her resentment does not lead her to abandon her child. If she is unable to be tender toward her husband, she is able to love him. Despite her history she has greater capacity for emotional relationships than most of the patients in this study.

During one of her last visits Agnes went from talking of her violent impulses to talking of her fears of cars, elevators, and airplanes. All of these fears seem related to her fear of losing control over her violent impulses and being violently punished for such loss of control. Suicide has the advantage of giving her at least illusory control over both her violence and her punishment.

When Betty Scott,* a thirty-one-year-old woman, jumped from the fourth-story window of her aunt's tenement apartment, she broke her right tibia and fibula. Soon

* No psychological tests were given to Betty Scott.

after her admission to the hospital Betty tried to end her life again by hanging herself from the traction bar over her head.

After leaving Tom, with whom she had lived for the past three years, she spent the last few nights with her aunt. The night she jumped, Betty awoke and became fearful when she thought she saw a shadow. She imagined that her aunt had let someone into the apartment. Becoming angry with her, Betty turned on the gas, planning to "blow up the place," but afraid that someone would smell the gas, she decided to jump. She says she knows her aunt would not let anyone hurt her but she can never trust anyone and wants vengeance for any hurt done to her. Although she feels she made her suicide attempt on the spur of the moment, Betty says she has had thoughts of suicide off and on for the last two years and had told her aunt the day before her attempt that something awful was going to happen. Betty says of Tom that she "worshipped the ground he walked on" for their first two years together. During the past year, however, they fought over his drinking, over his relations with other women, and over money. Betty says he would come home drunk and would beat her. She now tries unconvincingly to deny that her suicide attempt has anything to do with Tom.

Betty has been working as a maid while Tom, who works infrequently, shines shoes. He has told Betty that he gets money from another girl.

Betty has thought many times of killing Tom. He often talks of killing her and will playfully pull a tie around her neck. When he does she tells him she will kill him if he does not leave her alone. "He's lucky to be alive," she says, "beating me up and going to sleep like that." During the interviews she frequently returns to her fantasy of murdering him.

Admitting that she started many of her fights with Tom, Betty says she has always had a violent temper. At fourteen she threw a brick at a girl and caused her to be hospitalized. At eighteen she went after a boyfriend with a knife but he took it from her. Now she fights with both men and women and has twice gone home for a knife only to find her adversary gone when she returned. While Betty is generally depressed and says she has been that way most of her life, she seemed to come to life when discussing her past fights.

Some of her resentment of Tom has been elaborated in a paranoid manner. Betty feels that people are trying to poison her and that Tom is arranging her death. She thinks that friends of his may be poisoning her food in the hospital. While she knows this is only an "idea in my head," she nevertheless feels it to be so. Both she and Tom have actually threatened to poison each other, although Betty says she has never done anything about her threat.

Describing herself as never having been happy, Betty relates her childhood as a story of work and punishment. Her mother, a very strict woman, beat her severely for being fresh or disobedient. "I was lucky if I could walk for two weeks afterwards," she says. Her father worked, slept, and was indifferent to her. When telling how she had to get up every morning before school or work to take three younger siblings to her grandmother, Betty cries. She feels this should not have been her job. Although she was terrified of her mother as a child, she misses her now and tearfully wishes she would come from Alabama to visit her in the hospital. She feels her mother has changed and has become more understanding in recent years.

One night shortly after her admission to the hospital, Betty had the following dreams:

> She had a little girl with a dirty face. She told her to wash. Her grandmother said the girl was like her. She was hurt and decided to leave. The grandmother told her to leave and not come back.

Betty was shot and said to the person who had done it that he had shot the wrong person.

Tom was clearly the person who should have been shot. He had slapped her face in a bar prior to her leaving him. Talking of her grandmother led her to talk of her aunt's disapproval and her mother's mistreatment of her when she was a child. Betty sees herself as the little girl in the dream. Hurt and rejected by her grandmother (mother), she blames herself (the dirty face) and leaves in the dream much as she leaves Tom in her current life. To "leave and never come back" suggests killing herself. She connects Tom's slapping her face with her being rejected as a little girl for having a dirty face. There was suggestive but not conclusive evidence that the dirty face is also a derogatory reference to blackness and being Negro, a theme that will be considered in subsequent patients who express it more clearly.

In any case Betty's pain and anger over her current rejection awaken the pain and anger of her childhood rejection. Her fantasies of killing Tom are linked with her fantasies of killing her aunt (probably a substitute for her mother) by blowing up her place, but she decides to be the one "to leave" or do the rejecting by killing herself. Betty is as likely as Agnes Carreth to commit violence toward her man as she is to kill herself.

Betty is also similar to Agnes in the way in which hurt and anger over a man's rejection open up the pain and anger of earlier maternal rejection. Both their mothers used and denied them by forcing them at a premature age to care for younger siblings while giving them little in return. Betty came out of her childhood, however, with much more emotional constriction than Agnes. She is closer to Ina Tracy in showing most life when discussing her violence.

Like the previous patients, the next three women had great difficulty in controlling their violent impulses. They seem able to deal with homicidal and suicidal feelings only by making a sharp break with reality, often attributing these feelings to a series of hallucinatory voices that plague them. Only one of the three patients is completely successful in curbing her violence by this means, and she seems to be paying a particularly high price for her success. The integration of all three, although psychotic, is structured rather than chaotic. As much can be learned from understanding them as from any of the other patients in this study.

Alice Markens at twenty-three has had six children and looks ten years older. When she learned her husband, Ralph, was seeing another woman, she became "hot," hit him, and made a suicide attempt with twenty thorazine tablets. An hour later she changed her mind and told Ralph what she had done.*

Ralph, who is twenty-five, is a steady worker who has been employed in a shoe factory for the past three and a half years. They grew up in the same North Carolina town, where Alice, at fifteen, became pregnant with his child. After she had a miscarriage he went North. She followed him to New York, where she lived with her sister until she was seventeen. A year before their marriage she gave birth to their first child. Alice says that until a year ago Ralph was a quiet man who came home nights. Later she admitted that she had heard stories of

* Alice's story to one of the TAT cards suggests the fantasy that her husband will be sorry and remorseful after she is dead.

her husband's adventures with other women before that and felt some of them were probably true.

In describing arguments with her husband about money, Alice began to discuss her mother-in-law, who, she said, always interfered in the marriage and advised her son against spending money on his children. Alice described her mother-in-law's fatal illness, which occurred fifteen months before her suicide attempt. In an agonizing death from uremia her mother-in-law had convulsions during which Alice held down her hands and feet. Although Alice felt that her mother-in-law's death precipitated emotional difficulties that culminated in her brief hospitalization, she does not appear to be fully aware of the guilt she felt at what were most likely death wishes toward her mother-in-law.

Alice has become frightened of dying in a similar way. She had developed a "knot" in her stomach that felt as though the life in her were trying to come out; she thought that if it rose to her mouth (perhaps a reference to her anger) she would die. She began to feel that her own hands and feet were not part of her and had nightmares in which her mother-in-law came into her room and touched her covers. In another nightmare a boy who had died in an auto wreck came back and said he was not dead. They then went into a cave together. Alice feared the dead and seemed to feel they could cause her death.

During this same period Alice began to hear a coarse, rough male voice telling her to jump from the window or throw herself in front of a car. If she were home she would slam the window shut when the voice began to speak. When asked whose voice it could be, Alice said, with some surprise, that it was like her father's.

Her father's role in her present situation became more apparent when she began to talk about her childhood. When Alice said she did not have a father, her voice broke. She said he had left home when she was five because there was no work for him. For about a year he sent the family money. She remembers envying other children who talked about what they did with their fathers.

Alice was the seventh of eight children. She was cared for during the day by her older sisters while her mother worked in a peanut factory. Her mother came home to give them supper and never stayed out at night or ran around. "I will always love Mama, no matter what," Alice said. When asked whether "no matter what" suggested she had some reason not to love her mother, Alice admitted, "Well, she always preferred my sister Roseanne to me." Roseanne was three years older than Alice.

Throughout her childhood Alice fought with her sister Flora, who was two years older and whom she once pushed through a glass window. Alice felt that her mother was unfair to punish her since Flora had started the fight.

Alice fought more than her brothers and sisters and was often in disputes with girls outside of her family. Laughingly, she relates an incident in which she hit a girl with a stick. During this period Alice suffered from convulsive attacks with loss of consciousness. A year or two later, when she began going out with boys, her convulsions and fights stopped. As a child she had had occasional visions and recalls as most striking one she had at twelve in which she was visiting a hospital and saw a ball of fire come out of the wall and roll down the corridor into another hall. She also remembers seeing a headless man. In a current fantasy that will be discussed later Alice decapitates her husband. Of her visions she says, "Maybe they were only my imagination, but I saw them."

In discussing her anger and her efforts to control it, she was asked if she felt there was a fire inside her. She seemed to light up at once at this idea and says she felt she was fiery and would burn up all the time before she got nervous. In the past two years she feels she has become more depressed than angry.* Fire has played an even more literal role in her life. In an effort to force her husband to move she had once set a fire in her apartment. During the period before her first hospitalization Alice at times tried to pass off her anger by saying that she was "forgetful"—for example, "I was always burning supper or the baby's bottle." Although Alice has six children, only two sons, aged four and six, are now with her. The others were placed elsewhere when she was first hospitalized. From the period just before her hospitalization she recalled the following nightmares:

> She stole money and was running away. A policeman shot her and she felt herself dying.
>
> A man drowned. A woman was on a pier, watching. She was stabbed from behind by another man.

In the second dream she expresses herself passively—that is, he drowns and she is only watching. Whether her anger is expressed actively, as in the stealing of the first dream, or passively, as in the second, she needs to make sure she is punished.

Her associations to these dreams were clearly related to her fights with her husband over money. She had often hoped he would have an accident and die. When asked whether she had thought about killing him she answered, "At times I think like that—I'd like to cut his arms off, his head off, his . . . [she stops]. I'd like to tear him up right in my hands."

* The internalization of her anger is represented on the Rorschach test by such responses as "insides of a human body"—responses of poor form accuracy suggestive also of preoccupation with bodily functioning in the context of poor reality-testing ability. Gross perceptual distortions were apparent even on the relatively structured TAT, on which, for example, she perceived the boy-violin scene (Card I) as a picture of horses which the boy is looking at. On the SCT, where frequent responses were "cry" or "crying," the rather childlike nature of her response repertoire is also apparent.

A recent dream that followed her suicide attempt is perhaps more revealing of her ideas about death and suicide.

> She was in the house of a boy she knew years ago who had committed suicide. His mother had laid his clothes out on the stove. She wanted to peep at them. She recalled a black sweater with gray and white stripes. The boy or his voice appeared from out of the stove.

The boy was a playmate who had hanged himself in her home town in North Carolina when Alice was thirteen. Because he had been depressed his mother locked him in his room to prevent him from killing himself. He hanged himself on a night when she forgot to do so. The sweater in the dream actually belonged to her husband's brother, who, like her husband, drinks too much.

Her confusion over whom she wants dead, herself or her husband, seems to enter this dream. Although Alice says that as a Baptist she believes that the "good" go to heaven and that suicides are sinners who remain "in the ground," the voice from the oven is suggestive of a rebirth fantasy, particularly since she wanted to try on the boy's clothes. She goes on to say that she actively wishes she were a man because "they have fun, they can do what they want, while I have no fun."

Although her earliest and strongest memories centered on feeling neglected or rejected by her mother in favor of the other children, Alice never expressed open anger toward her mother or ever argued with her. "You don't sass your mother," she says. In the hospital she dreamed that she was happy jumping and shouting in her mother's church. In reality she goes to church only occasionally and never to revival meetings. The dream seemed to be an attempt to reconcile with her mother by doing things her way. Alice also did not "sass" me or the therapist who began treating her at the hospital. She was depressed and reluctant to talk but was nevertheless polite. She missed several outpatient appointments, later explaining that she "gets the shakes" talking to me. She seemed to fear that talking about her feelings would lessen her control over them.

As a child the anger that pervaded Alice's life was expressed in her frequent street fighting. Her convulsions probably represented some attempt to internalize and control this anger. It might be noted here that a history of frequent street fights in childhood was characteristic of most of the patients, female and male, in the study. While this must be seen in the context of an environment in which such fighting is frequent, these patients fought much more than their friends and siblings did.

Alice sees her father and men in general as freer to express anger and as having more fun than women but, while she has fantasies of such freedom, she sees it as leading only to self-destruction for her. The hallucination of her father's voice telling her to kill herself appears to be not merely a dramatic expression of her feelings concerning his abandonment of her but is also a warning of the danger to her of following in his footsteps by expressing anger toward her mother.

While Alice's violent reaction to her husband's rejection and her freedom in fantasizing cutting him into pieces are similar to the responses of the last few patients, her feeling that "you don't sass your mother" is quite different from what has been seen up to now. The need not to be angry with her mother suggests the degree to which she feels dependent on her mother. Alice's anger toward her mother-in-law and her guilt over this anger after her mother-in-law died threaten her control over the fire she feels inside her. Her somatic and hypochondriacal symptoms, as well as her suicide attempt, are best understood as her current efforts to internalize this anger.

Alice has the same unconscious conflict with the control of violent impulses as the previous patients. She is more than usually threatened both by loss of control and by recognition of the source of her anger and needs to make a greater break with reality than the previous patients in order to maintain her adaptation.

After swallowing half an ounce of rat poison containing 79 per cent arsenic, twenty-nine-year-old Glenda Williams lay down to die in her hotel room. She became sick, vomited, had pains in her stomach, and called for help.

Glenda was reluctant to talk about her feelings and was vague when she did so but she does say that "voices" have been telling her to kill herself on and off for the last four years. During one of several stays in state mental hospitals over the past few years she swallowed cigarette ashes (with no ill effect) in response to voices telling her to kill herself. At the time of her present attempt she had become tired of the voices and of the problems involved in working and caring for herself, although she has been receiving welfare aid for the past six months.

Born in South Carolina, Glenda has no memory of her mother or father. She was told by her grandmother, aunt, and cousin, who took turns at raising her, that her parents died when she was a child, but voices have told her that only her father is dead and that her mother is alive in an insane asylum. Glenda's first memory in life is sitting in a highchair questioning such voices about the people in the house and receiving an answer from them.

When Glenda was sixteen or seventeen she had an ectopic pregnancy but managed to finish high school. She married at twenty but left her husband two years later to come to New York because he drank, hit her, stayed out, and told her he had other women. On the train to New

York the voices became disturbing for the first time—they told her to kill a man on the train, "who they said was no good." Since then they have plagued her by saying that there are snakes lurking around her, that the aunt and cousin who raised her did not like her, and that she should drink or take dope.*

Glenda is preoccupied with her fears of snakes, black spiders, mice, and rats. In the past she has had hallucinations in which snakes and rats talk to her; in the hospital she imagined that black spiders were coming toward her bed. When questioned about her having taken rat poison, Glenda explained that her former husband had become angry with her during their marriage and had swallowed some. She went on to talk of her fear of snakes and rats, commenting that they "must be on earth for something, same as me." Since Glenda had stressed the animals' viciousness, she was asked if she saw herself that way. "No," she answered, "but the voices want me to be vicious, to kill people, to say whatever comes to my mind."

Since Glenda had also stressed the animals' blackness, she was asked whether this would refer to being Negro. "It could be," she said. "The voices tell me they will change me into someone white." Glenda went on to talk of voices promising to make her white and a man. Glenda also has fantasies of rebirth as a white man, a transformation she feels would free her to do what she wants.

Glenda says she is not a person who expresses anger or becomes violent when annoyed, but when very angry she shakes all over and becomes weak.† Nevertheless she

* Psychological tests confirmed the overt nature of her thinking disturbance. The quality of her thinking was revealed by such responses as that given to the WAIS question, "Why are people who are born deaf usually unable to talk?" She responded, "I don't know if the ear organ is connected to the neck."

† While aggressive imagery was revealed on the Rorschach test (Card II, "two warriors"; Card VI, "some kind of Indian weapons"), the reported expressions of hostility were low in contrast to a high guilt score on the Hostility Inventory.

sees herself as a vicious black animal to be most appropriately exterminated by rat poison. She connects her "viciousness" with her blackness. To her, being white means not only freedom but also freedom from destructiveness.

The "voices" that tell Glenda that the women who raised her did not like her probably express the true state of affairs and suggest the source of her anger. She resembles Alice Markens in her inability to accept anger toward the women who raised her. She is even more threatened than Alice by her anger and avoids angry eruptions in general by projecting them into her hallucinations or dealing with them through her animal phobias. These symptoms have served some integrative function, which now seems to be breaking down, so that she views suicide as the only way left to deal with what she regards as her destructiveness.

Lorrie Peters, a light brown girl of twenty, had made several suicide attempts over the past three years during periods of depression, which were usually accompanied by outbursts of violence. During each episode Lorrie talked of wanting to kill someone: her father, her sister Mary, Mary's boyfriend, and her own boyfriend.

During one episode Lorrie had an hallucination in which a sailor she knew three years earlier told her to follow him out the window. She felt he wanted her to kill herself, but she refused, saying she would kill him instead. On another occasion, however, she did try to jump out the window and was stopped by her sister. Another time she attacked this sister with a can opener. Lorrie has had to be hospitalized during these episodes, and after each hospitalization she returns home to her parents in Georgia. Becoming bored, she comes back to New York to live with her two older sisters, Irene and Mary. Irene has always been to some degree a mother surrogate for Lorrie.

Two nights before her present suicide attempt, while spending the night with Alvin, a young man she has been involved with for the past two months, Lorrie had the following dream:

> Her brother was shot in the stomach. He was carried on a stretcher to mother. He got up and walked.

Lorrie's brother is in Vietnam. She connects the idea that his injury would bring about his return to her mother with her own current desire to return to her. Her sisters are not in favor of her going home again; when Lorrie was asked why she does not go anyway, she replied, "I always listen to my sister Irene."

She goes on to talk about Alvin, saying that she cannot take him seriously because of her Navy boyfriend. She admits that she finds him entertaining, that she can talk to him, and that he satisfies her sexually, and concedes the possibility that she is fantasizing about the sailor to avoid becoming too involved with Alvin. She seems threatened by the closeness with him and angry with him for it. It seems likely that he, as well as Lorrie, is represented in her dream of her brother being shot. Closeness to Alvin threatens Lorrie's dependent tie to her sister Irene and to her mother.

Lorrie was born in a Georgia city, and is the youngest of five children. Her violent temper dates back to her childhood when she fought in particular with her father, who she felt was meaner to her than to the other children. Lorrie's mother was generally withdrawn but was subject to temper outbursts, similar to Lorrie's, in which she would strike her children. Despite Lorrie's temper, she could never display, and found it hard to discuss, her anger toward her mother. Lorrie's difficulties when she is away from home and her extreme dependence on her mother make this seem less surprising.

At the beginning of her stay in the hospital Lorrie was also dependent in a childlike way, as well as talkative, friendly, and ingratiating. As time progressed it became evident that these attitudes inadequately defended her against her rage. She provoked fights on the ward and physically attacked one of the patients. She expressed in her interviews the fear of losing control and killing someone. Lorrie's rage and her fears of retaliation make her world a frightening one. She has nightmares in which she fears snakes and says she is terrified of being alone because she fears rape, murder, and kidnapping.

Lorrie's religious beliefs play an important role in her efforts at adaptive control. She wore a Star of David and explained that Irene and she are Hebrew. Irene had first converted from being a Methodist and influenced Lorrie to convert as well. She does not like to be called Jewish because people think Jewish means white, and she explains that one can be both black and Hebrew. "I am black, not Negro," Lorrie says. "I'm proud of it. 'Negro' is a white man's word. If I let myself think of the injustices to my ancestors, I would be prejudiced and mad. I don't let myself think of it. I don't want to be mad."

Much of Lorrie's explanation of her religious belief is circumstantial and confused. While in the hospital Lorrie had a dream in which her Negro rabbi told her to remember what he had said. She connects this with his telling her to study the Bible to find out who she is. She has done this and decided that she was Rachel. She feels both Rachel and she are disturbed and have been helped by changing their religion.

Lorrie's faith includes a belief in reincarnation: in a new life she would like to be a dog. A dog's ability to accept a submissive dependence is in striking contrast to Lorrie's angry struggle with her own dependent cravings.

Both Lorrie's mother and father serve as models for her violent outbursts. She is like all the patients in this chapter in the difficulty she has in controlling violent impulses. She is most like Alice Markens and Glenda Williams in being unable to deal with her anger toward her mother and needing a severe break with reality, including hallucinations, to cope with her fears of losing control and killing someone.

The frustration and rage of the suicidal black women is as striking as that of the men. The impression that the black female suffers less than the male because racial institutions strike so directly at the male's image of himself as a worker and provider is not borne out by the case histories. The most disastrous impact of racial institutions seems to be felt so early in life and so overwhelmingly that the plight of the female seems as bad as that of the male. Frustration, rage, and violence already characterize the lives of both sexes when they are teenagers, and there is little difference between men and women in the degree of despair that is so often present by the time they are young adults. While the male is harder hit by socio-economic pressure, it is often the female who bears the brunt of his anger.

It should be noted that while the rage of most of the patients has its source in maternal frustration, and their mothers are blamed by most of them for their misfortunes, their fathers, who have often totally rejected them, are usually allowed to escape criticism or anger. Their mothers have evidently been the source of enough security and gratification to arouse expectations—expectations that they have frustrated or failed to fulfill. Their fathers, in contrast, are often seen as figures of whom nothing is expected.

It should also be kept in mind that the maternal deprivation observed so often in the ghetto is itself the product of the racial institutions that govern the lives of black people. While it is often of primary importance for the individual subject, subsequent cases and the concluding chapter will hopefully make clear that from a psychosocial point of view maternal deprivation is but a link in a chain.

In any case, the violence that is set in motion by a series of events, usually beginning with maternal frustration, ends with a feeling of being trapped in an unchangeable life situation. Whether the individual acts on homicidal impulses, tries to drown them in alcohol, "cools" them by emotional detachment, controls them through religious faith, projects them as hallucinations or turns all feeling inward in suicide, the picture that emerges of young black adults struggling with conscious murderous impulses is a far different picture than emerges from most studies of white suicide. It is also a picture in sharp contrast to conventional theoretical descriptions of the relation between suicide and violence.

It is now fifty years since Freud wrote of suicide as deriving from "unconscious hostility toward a lost loved object." He described in the psychoanalytic language of his time how the individual incorporates and identifies with the person that is lost and turns the anger he feels toward that person back on himself. According to this formulation, suicide is an inverted homicide, the outgrowth of the unconscious desire to kill someone else.

Freud's valuable insight has been modified, so that today it is seen as only one of a half-dozen psychodynamic explanations that can underlie suicide. Moreover, observations by both anthropologists and psychoanalysts have shown that the psychodynamics of suicide vary from culture to culture, so that in both primitive and civilized cultures there is striking variation in the meaning, significance, and frequency of suicide.

Unfortunately sociological attempts to utilize Freud's work in dealing with society as a whole have tended toward rigid propositions concerning a supposed inverse relationship between suicide and homicide that ignores social and cultural differences in attitudes toward life as well as death. Henry and Short in particular have worked diligently to utilize this supposed inverse relationship between suicide and homicide in the hope of explaining both.* They confine their interpretation of data to the United States, stating that a cross-cultural frame of reference would "confuse" the picture. Indeed it would.

In fact, while there are countries high in suicide and low in homicide (Denmark) and countries high in homicide and low in suicide (Italy), there are also countries high in homicide and high in suicide (Finland), and countries like Norway that are low in both.

Furthermore, individuals who commit homicide have a high subsequent suicide rate, while individuals who kill themselves have a higher than average percentage of homicide in their prior histories. But this is not too significant, since virtually any form of psychosocial pathology—drug addiction, alcoholism, suicide, crime, etc.—will have a higher than average correlation with any other form. Such a correlation only shows that people in difficulty are apt to express the difficulty in more than one way and makes somewhat foolish the efforts to formularize relationships between suicide and other forms of psychosocial pathology.

Henry and Short summarize their work as follows:

* Andrew Henry and James Short, *Suicide and Homicide* (Glencoe, Ill.: The Free Press, 1954).

A person of low status is required to conform to the demands and expectations of persons of higher status merely by virtue of his low status. A person involved in intense "social" interaction with another person is required to conform to the demands and expectations imposed as a condition of the relationship.

These observations may be summarized in the following proposition: the strength of external restraint to which behavior is subjected varies positively with the strength of the relational system and inversely with position in the status hierarchy. "Strength of external restraint" is defined as the degree to which behavior is required to conform to the demands and expectations of other persons.

Our empirical propositions relating suicide and homicide to status and strength of the relational system may now be restated in terms of the strength of external restraint as follows: suicide varies negatively and homicide positively with the strength of external restraint over behavior.*

If the uninitiated reader has the patience to reread those three paragraphs until they become clear, he will have mastered an example of the formularized, simplistic thinking that has characterized much of the sociological approach to suicide. One does not need to go to other cultures or even to the Negro subculture to refute such theorems. Unskilled laborers and farm workers, who are at the bottom of the status scale in the United States, should have the lowest suicide rates in the culture. Unfortunately for them and this theory, they have the highest.

In the young adult Negro group described it is clear that there is a relation, and not an inverse one, between suicide and homicide. This is based in the particular

* *Ibid.*, p. 17.

black experience in our culture, an experience that generates violence within the Negro and presents him with the problem of controlling it.

The alternation among these young blacks between conscious, overt violence and self-destructive behavior is a far cry from "the unconscious hostility toward the lost loved object" described by Freud. Patients fitting the picture Freud described are usually anything but openly destructive. The statistics mentioned in the first chapter showing that the high peaks of Negro homicide and suicide occur during the same age period (twenty to thirty-five) take on more meaning when it is seen that underlying suicide as well as homicide is the central common factor of the attempt by the young black population to deal with its rage and violence.

3

Suicide and Male Homosexuality

THE black male suicidal patients who were homosexual illustrate more than merely a very different way of trying to avoid violent impulses. These patients (three now to be discussed as well as the first patient in the study) show how the pressures on the black family operate to handicap the male and cause him to hate his race, his sex, and himself.

A month after his mother had locked him out of their apartment, twenty-year-old Leroi Nifson cut his left forearm in an attempt to end his life. His act was the climax of four weeks of drifting from friend to friend and sleeping in a park. Five months earlier Leroi had tried to kill himself by taking eighteen sleeping pills in a Lower East Side park. He now feels he no longer wants to die but "would rather turn to things outside himself."

Leroi says he is dependent on his mother even though they do not get along. He blames his fights with her for his earlier suicide attempt. Critical of Leroi's hippy clothes and bracelets, his communist political interests, and his Muslim religion, she has torn his picture of Mao Tse-tung from the wall, becomes angry when he listens to opera on the radio, and has made him feel she resents his intelligence and taste.

The fight that caused his mother to lock him out was about Leroi's demand for a Muslim diet: meatless meals served on separate dishes. Discord between Leroi and his mother has caused her to lock him out twice before. But he says he will not go home as he has in the past after a few hours of feeling lonesome and afraid. Leroi refused to see his mother or the other members of his family while he was in the hospital, yet he tried to deny being upset or angry with them.

Leroi's father was born in New York, his mother in Syria. Leroi was born and raised in a black community in New York City. During fierce arguments his father often assaulted his mother; seven years ago he deserted her. Since Mr. Nifson returned a year ago, the fights have resumed. A violent man, he was arrested once for assault in an argument away from home and, in the current lockout, he threw a flower pot from his window at Leroi who was on the street below.

Leroi's mother beat him until he was fourteen or fifteen, when she began to fear him. While he is never violent, he stands up to her, unlike his brothers and sisters. Although she used to rule with an "iron fist," Leroi feels he is now able to counter her blows verbally since he can out-talk her.

Leroi was bright in school, but was unruly and dropped out in the seventh grade. Since then he has divided his time between educating himself, stealing, experimenting with drugs, and homosexuality. In the past two years Leroi has had three jobs: he worked as a messenger in the garment district for one week and quit; he washed dishes for one day and quit; and he worked as a clerk for three months and quit. He says he does not feel he can get ahead fast enough at work. When he was eligible to go to an Urban League College preparatory course, however, he failed to begin. He blames his non-attendance on lack of money and his unstable life with his mother.

Although Leroi recalls that when he was eleven he liked to dress in his mother's clothes, his overt homosexual activity started four or five years later. Now he picks up young white or Puerto Rican men and takes them to a hotel room, for which he pays. He performs fellatio on them and has an orgasm while doing so. He says he prefers little men of the size he was when he began his homosexual activity. His contacts do not last more than one night.

Disturbed at being asked why he excludes Negroes from his homosexual contacts, Leroi denied prejudice and eventually explained that he considers himself Arabic and not Negro; a white man who is sympathetic to the Negro cause. Of a medium-brown color, Leroi concedes that everyone treats him as though he were black and his brothers and sisters all consider themselves Negro. His mother does not identify herself as an Arab. Leroi says he regards the penis as a warm and nurturing breast. Since his mother's breast is white, he explains, maybe he needs a white penis.

Leroi has never made any attempt at heterosexual relations. He says women talk too much, will not let people alone, and are always critical. He feels all girls are, like his mother, given to ridicule and contempt. Blaming her for turning him into a homosexual, Leroi says she made him fear women.

Leroi wants a life that has "no place for emotion." Wanting to be "political," "cool," and "calculating," he tries to destroy his moments of anger by thinking of an algebra equation until the feeling passes. He uses his intelligence as an angry weapon against his mother, beating her verbally in a manner that seems akin to his father's beating her physically. With me as well he attempts to answer all questions intellectually—an attempt that gives his speech a mannered quality.* Unlike most of the other patients Leroi did not engage in actual fighting. Nevertheless he feels violence is justified as a form of political action. He says his politics are racial and that he is against Europeans. He favors a violent policy by the Arabs toward Israel (his mother does not), by the Communist Chinese toward the Russians, and by the most ardent of the black power advocates toward the white community.

When Leroi says he no longer wants to die but "would rather turn to things outside himself," it is militant black power politics that he has in mind. His militancy helps him to harness and channel anger that otherwise would be more personally overwhelming in a destructive or self-destructive way. While Leroi tries to use black nationalism to feel superior to whites and blacks alike, his passivity, his dependency, his sexual fears, and his work failures all indicate that this attitude is but a thinly veiled compensatory attempt to deny his feeling of inadequacy.

Like Peter Churney, Leroi can picture himself committing violence on a mass scale while remaining cool and aloof. Neither of them can endure the subjective feeling of anger, but angry or destructive behavior without this feeling seems to gratify the impulse without the discomfort of emotion.†

The violence that has been described as permeating Negro life operates in a particular way with Leroi and Peter to move them in the direction of homosexuality. From their fathers' treatment of their mothers they have

* On the psychological tests Leroi also uses intellectualization as a compensatory way of handling feelings of unacceptability and inferiority. Deep-rooted feelings of rejection and pervasive passivity were indicated. In spite of his "average" IQ (103), his vocabulary is at the very superior level and suggests a much higher potential than he is currently attaining.

† Both patients are among the lowest on Hostility Inventory scores.

derived a conception of masculinity and male sexuality that is frighteningly violent and to be avoided. In Leroi's nightmares he usually runs from a man who seems to represent his father, himself, or both. The fathers of both Peter and Leroi tended to alternate between being present and violent and being absent; they present a contrast to the more usual totally absent father. Leroi's detached, somewhat schizoid adaptation was severely disrupted only when his father returned and further strained his uneasy relationship with his mother.

Both Leroi and Peter see their mothers as cold, severe, and rejecting, and for both of them frustration with their mothers is the source of much of their rage. Both blame their mothers' excessive control and criticism for making them fear women and turning them into homosexuals, and both of them remain attached to their mothers in an angry dependent way. Leroi's dependency runs the gamut from using Muslim dietary laws to try to force his mother to feed him as he wants to be fed, to being precipitated into a suicide attempt after being "locked out" by her.

Another aspect of the mother's role in the black family operates in a more definable way to encourage a homosexual adaptation in a boy already frightened by a violent conception of heterosexuality. The Negro homosexual subjects tended to be most uneasy and uncomfortable when discussing relations their mothers had with other men after being abandoned by their fathers. Leroi is particularly reluctant to discuss any relationships his mother had while his father was away.

The father's abandonment and the mother's sexual activity often made her seem an available sexual object, making the need to avoid heterosexuality all the greater. Their need to protect themselves against temptation and their view of heterosexuality as violent combine to produce a recurring double bind in the Negro homosexual patients. Leroi and Peter are typical in tending to handle their relationships with their mothers by identifying with them and remaining attached to them in a dependent, emasculated manner.

Leroi's attempt to identify racially as well as sexually with a non-Negro mother is a factor that differentiates him from Peter. He becomes involved sexually only with white men, makes an equation between the penis and the breast, and says he needs a white penis as a substitute for his mother's breast. More important, he insists that he is white and an Arab, and merely chooses to identify with the Negro cause.

Leroi's need to be white and to feel superior to blacks and whites has been discussed in connection with his Muslim beliefs. Blackness for him is associated with his angry self-hatred. The fellatio he performs on white men can well be seen as an attempt to incorporate their whiteness. As subsequent cases will make clearer, however, preference for a white partner is common in black homosexuals who do not have Leroi's interracial background.

Andrew Vallen, a dark, handsome, but somewhat effeminate nineteen-year-old, was admitted to the hospital after slashing his wrists with a razor blade. In discussing his suicide attempt Andrew mentions his difficulties at work, with his mother, and with homosexuality.

One week before his suicide attempt Andrew left the Job Corps, which he had entered for clerical training a month earlier. When he found that clerical training was not available he switched to cooking, which he came to dislike. Andrew also felt mistreated by the boys in the dorms, claiming that they teased him about his big lips.

Andrew is upset by his fights with his mother. On a visit to her house three days before his suicide attempt he was angered by the unexpected presence of his aunt. "I hadn't wanted her there," he said. "I came to see my mother."

Having begun homosexual activity when he was eleven or twelve, Andrew now blames most of his depression on this problem. He has maintained relationships with two young men over a five- or six-year period. Neither knows about the other. "I'm good at keeping secrets," he says sarcastically and bitterly. He blames his homosexuality on people in the neighborhood who predicted that he would become homosexual, that he would take after his homosexual uncle who lived with the family. When challenged about this explanation, Andrew became quite angry, saying, "You don't know how mean people can be."

Both of his relationships are with Puerto Rican boys of his own age. Denying any racial prejudice in this choice, he says he has always liked what is new and different. His sexual activity consists of his being penetrated anally. He never has an erection or orgasm until he masturbates by himself afterward. He feels disgusted and humiliated by his homosexual activity and says he engages in it because he does not care about himself.

Two years ago, Andrew made an attempt at intercourse with a girl his own age. He says he lost his erection but attributes this partly to her talking about his "big lips." Blaming his big lips for his inability to approach girls, he says he wants an operation that will make them thinner. Denying that he associates big lips with being Negro, he says, "I'm proud I am Negro." He has non-sexual fantasies of a girl he knew from his fifteenth to his seventeenth year. Andrew says they planned to marry but she died from a malignant tumor. When questioned about sexual activity with her, he said angrily that he had too much respect for her. "A beautiful relationship is more than that," he said. Asked if he felt that sex was part of a relationship, he again became angry and said, "It has to be if you wish children."

Andrew is an only child born and raised in New York.

When he was five years old his parents separated, obtaining a divorce when he was seven. Andrew rarely sees his father and has no wish to see him now.

After his parents' divorce Andrew lived with his mother, uncle, grandmother, and two aunts. Except for a few months after his birth Andrew's mother worked for the welfare department. Although he said she was a social worker and is now a supervisor, his mother stated that she has always been a clerical worker for the department. While his mother worked he was raised by his two aunts, with whom he did not get along. His mother encouraged him to do a good deal of housework—that is, washing and ironing. In recent years they have fought over his unwillingness to continue doing these chores.

Andrew says he has a bad temper. He has fought frequently with his mother, uncle, and aunts and has hit all of them at least once. When someone spilled milk on him in the hospital, he was "almost forced to bust him in the mouth." Andrew estimates he has had one hundred fights. He frequently became irritable and angry with me, making such remarks as, "People are always forcing me to talk about things I don't wish to talk about."* To keep his temper under control Andrew carries a zippered Bible with him and zips back and forth when he thinks of punching someone.

Andrew's father also had a hot temper and beat his wife often. Despite this, Andrew blamed her for allowing his father to beat him. After a beating that required that he be taken to the hospital, his mother did strike his father. His father would go out drinking and visiting

* The psychological tests suggest the possibility that his very great hostility may be a defense against his passivity. (His violent reaction to being held up may support this.) His desire for a completely passive state is implied in his SCT completion, *I feel happiest when:* "I'm asleep," a motivation which suggested to the tester the possibility of suicide as the alternative resolution of his difficulties. On the SCT he made many references to his guilt and depression over being "gay."

other women until his mother finally told him not to come back. Andrew's first memory of his father concerns his father's temper and is significant in understanding his father's role in Andrew's retreat from heterosexual activity. When he was three or four his father had promised to take him to a ball game. He was playing with a girl and began chasing her. When his father saw him he beat him and did not take him to the ball game.

When Andrew reached the eleventh grade in school he had difficulty with mathematics and dropped out. He began working as a clerk in an insurance firm but lost his job after four months because his drinking made him miss too many days. Before going into the Job Corps he was unemployed and lived on what his mother gave him.

When he was seventeen Andrew made a similar suicide attempt shortly before his mother remarried. He insists that the two events were only coincidentally related. He says that he wanted her to remarry and could have stopped her if he disapproved. He feels he tried to end his life because he was tired of hurting his mother with his homosexual activity and his street fighting.

After ten months of living away from home Andrew moved home a month before he entered the Job Corps because he felt he wanted to be with his mother. Now he prefers to live away from her. Andrew goes from talking about leaving his mother to talking about giving up homosexuality.

Three weeks before his admission to the hospital Andrew decided to break off his homosexual relations and registered for treatment at a mental hygiene center, where he was put on a waiting list. Both the boys he had been involved with surprised him by agreeing to end their relationships with him. During his stay in the hospital Andrew was angered by questions about homosexuality, insisting that for him it was a thing of the past.

In the hospital Andrew had one dream: he was singing

rock-and-roll songs but then began to sing spirituals. Andrew has started going back to church. He had once sung in the choir but became irritated when people said his choir singing was a sign of his being homosexual. He had wanted to be a rock-and-roll singer but now he feels he can put his voice to better use. In his church group there is a girl who has been influential in persuading him to give up fighting and homosexuality. He feels the Bible and his religion will help him to end both. He denies that his attempt to move away from both homosexual activity and his relationship with his mother played any part in his suicide attempt. His dream, however, suggests that his effort is costing him greatly in the loss of enjoyment and spontaneity. He seems to be making an attempt at an asexual identity that will undoubtedly be difficult or impossible to maintain.

Andrew's experience with a violent father who beat both him and his mother is similar to that of Peter Churney and Leroi Nifson. His own rage, like theirs, stems largely from feelings of maternal rejection and frustration. Andrew struggles mightily to avoid overt outbreaks of violence, but he is much more openly angry than Peter or Leroi and makes no effort to deny the subjective feeling of anger. Yet his struggle to avoid identifying with his father and his father's violence in particular leads him to reject his sex and his race.

He insists he is proud to be a Negro, but belies this assertion with his insistence on white homosexual partners and his preoccupation with an operation to thin his lips. He blames his thick lips—that is, his being Negro—for everything from sexual failure to difficulties in finding suitable work. It is clear, however, that Andrew needs to punish himself by such failures. In equating violence, blackness, and potency Andrew needs to attack all three elements in himself; his projected operation can be seen as symbolizing both racial and sexual castration.

Andrew's sexual passivity parallels his general passivity; it serves much like his fantasied operation as a self-castration directed against violence, blackness, and potency. While his need for a white partner seems similar to Leroi's, it is actually much more self-punitive. He feels humiliated, degraded, and depressed by his contacts and achieves orgasm only later by masturbating. The non-sexual nature of his fantasies of a former girlfriend suggests that she is a substitute for his mother. The beating Andrew takes from his homosexual activities suggests the beatings he took from his father for, among other things, running after a little girl. For Andrew, Leroi, and Peter, a father's violence was a great source of sexual intimidation. The beatings which all three boys shared with their mothers served to strengthen a sense of identification between the boys and their mothers. That Andrew's mother encouraged him in non-masculine activities further tightened the bond between them. Moreover, Andrew's father was unfaithful to his mother; Andrew's homosexual adaptation insures that he will never do likewise.

Andrew senses intuitively that giving up his mother and giving up homosexuality are one and the same thing. He angrily tries, like Leroi and Peter, to deny his dependency on his mother much as he tries to insist that his homosexuality is a thing of the past.

Andrew's latest suicide attempt was precipitated by a fight with his mother as well as by his attempt to give up homosexuality. His attempt four years ago was precipitated by her impending marriage. Now he seems to be making an even more determined effort to give up homosexuality and his mother even if it kills him. He is hoping to use the church not just as Leroi did, in an effort to curb his violence (his zippered Bible has served that function in the past), but as a replacement for his mother and homosexuality as well.

At thirty-eight Benjamin Ellis is a tall, dark, well-built, handsome man who wanted help because of his "anxiety, frustration, and loneliness." He has made three suicide attempts over the years, the last occurring only a few months ago when he set fire to his apartment after a violent argument with his wife. Intoxicated at the time, Ben was throwing things around the room and thinks he must have knocked over an ashtray and accidentally started a fire. After ringing a fire alarm, he went to the psychiatric outpatient department of a hospital and swallowed a solution containing codeine while waiting for a doctor. After this not very serious suicide attempt, he was kept in the hospital for ten days and then faced arson charges, for which he was placed on probation.

At first Ben spoke of his life as though all of his problems stemmed from his ten-year marriage; he is currently separated from his wife for the fifth time. Resigned and bitter, Ben says his wife never considered him or the children, insulted him and his family, and only wanted him so that he could take care of her material needs.

Although he is severely depressed over his marriage, Ben admits to talking about it so as to avoid discussing his homosexual activity. He said he wanted to tell me his "life story" so I could better understand how this problem had developed.

Ben was born in Virginia of unmarried parents. When his mother became pregnant his father abandoned her, forcing her to go to work and leave Ben to be raised by various aunts. When he was about five years old his mother became pregnant again and sent him and his older sister to live with his aunt in New York. After the birth of his youngest sister his mother joined them. In his early years he knew his mother as "Miss Ida" and did not call her "Mother" until one of her boyfriends persuaded him to. Only in the past year has he felt any love for his mother. "I blamed her that I was born out of wedlock," he said. "She left the children to accept life as she did—in the dark. Children were to be seen and not heard. I learned through self-experience. Seldom a full year at home—one aunt or another."

Ben went on to describe their drab life in a cold-water flat where they often slept three in a bed and subsisted on welfare. Of his childhood he said, "I used to wander around looking for something. I don't know what. I was hit by a car and a bus several times. I never took an active part as far as sports were concerned. I was never anxious to fight. Always sitting, looking. People tried to get me to do things, but no one really encouraged me. No one really was close to me except one uncle and he died. Never had too much to do with the outside world. I'd be in the movies or in the house or at times in the park. People came over—they were happier to see my sisters than me—they patted me on the head—never any real interest in me."

He blames his homosexuality on the women in his family, saying they did not care for baby boys or men. "To get along with them," he added, "you had to be submissive. They made me too weak to be a man. No one told me about myself as a man." Speaking of his mother's preference for his two sisters, Ben recalls that it led him to wish that he had been a girl.

At eleven or twelve he slept in the same bed with the uncle he liked and became aware of a fearful interest in physical contact with him. His first actual experience came at thirteen or fourteen, when an elderly man approached him. He went to the man's room, had fellatio performed on him, and was given money. He went back regularly although, when the man saw how interested he was, he stopped paying him. Ben remembers his anxiety at not seeing the man when he wanted to.

During this same period he remembers discovering his mother having sexual relations with a man. "It jarred me so much I wept," he said. Similarly, he remembers spying on his older sister and her husband while they were having sexual relations. He says it disturbed him since he did not think people did things like that.

When his mother moved, Ben lived for a while with another aunt. He slept on the same couch with her eighteen-year-old adopted son, Charles. "This triggered off a relationship," Ben explains. Charles inserted his penis into Ben's rectum and while Ben had no orgasm he looked for opportunities to repeat the experience. No word of their sexual relationship ever passed between them, and Ben felt "it was like it never happened." Charles, however, would ask Ben to do favors for him because of their sexual contacts. When Charles fell in love with a girl his affair with Ben came to an end. "I got angry," Ben said. "I did something awfully bad. Do you want to know what? He was dodging the draft board. I called them up. I felt if I couldn't have him, she couldn't. I had to live with it. If he hadn't returned I'd have had to live with it. He was OK, however."

Ben joined the Coast Guard in the hope that the service would cure his homosexuality. At eighteen, after boot training, he had his first heterosexual experience with a childhood girlfriend. She was married and her husband, who was in the Army, had "turned to the gay life." Ben went once to a hotel with her where they had sexual relations four times. He found it exhausting, felt he knew nothing about women, and wondered whether pleasing a woman required having sexual relations four times.

Ben became sexually involved with a married man

at his camp, then with another man who was engaged. His activity involved being penetrated anally or performing fellatio. Becoming involved with several men at the same time, Ben felt ashamed, brooded about his activity, and says he wished he were dead. He drank a bottle of iodine, was shipped to Ellis Island, and was discharged from the service.

When he came home he went to school to learn cooking, baking, and cake decorating. He did well in school but found it hard to get a job afterward. He has generally had to work as a hospital orderly.

Ben became sexually involved with a man who was courting his younger sister. When she married him, Ben futilely begged his mother to ask them to live elsewhere. One New Year's his sister discovered Ben and her husband in bed together and went to her mother. Ben left home. "I was hurt," he said. "I wished I was dead—felt I'd do anything not to be alive." When his sister died two years later, Ben claims that he felt terrible.

After leaving home Ben had several homosexual and heterosexual relationships. The latter involved older women he met through relatives and saw for his family's sake, he explains, so they would know there was a woman in his life. He would engage in sexual relations with them but with little or no pleasure.

While becoming more involved homosexually, he became more depressed with the homosexual way of life. He had several casual experiences which particularly depressed him. As an escape from homosexuality and depression, he began to think of marriage and religion.

Ben met his wife when they were both members of the Jehovah's Witnesses for a three-year period. He claims they married "accidentally" when, while discussing marriage in general, she took his remarks as a proposal and accepted. Before the marriage Ben was upset. "The closer it got," he said, "the more frustrated I got. I lost my job. I got sick. She wouldn't postpone it." Nevertheless, he claims that while he was "hysterically happy" after the marriage, and gave up homosexuality, his wife became depressed. With her first pregnancy serious difficulties between them began, and eventually he returned to homosexuality. He was, however, involved with another woman during one of their separations.

Ben sees his children only occasionally because it is "too much trouble" to visit them. He dreams that he is arguing with his second daughter, Barbara, who accuses him of not loving her enough; he agrees. He caused Barbara's birth by puncturing his contraceptive in the hope that the birth of another child would reconcile him and his wife. Instead, they separated right after her birth and he likes Barbara least of all his children, although he is not close to any of them. Yet one of the conditions he set in order to grant his wife a divorce is that he have her large picture of the children, raising the question whether he does not prefer the picture to the children.

Ben's sister has a daughter who is married to a twenty-five-year-old man who lives with the family. Ben and his nephew drink together and seem close to sexual involvement. Although he rejects the idea "out of respect for my niece and myself," an involvement with his nephew would be consistent for Ben. From turning Charles over to the draft board because he was planning to marry, to sleeping with his sister's husband or his friend's wife, he has repeatedly managed to come between men and women.

During the interviews Ben had a sexual encounter with a man he met in a public bathroom. Ben felt dirty after the experience, explaining, "I do things with men, don't with women because men are dirty anyhow. The man was Negro and not as clean as he could be." After their first sexual contact, Ben insisted they take a bath.

Ben now began to discuss Roger, a man with whom he is still sexually involved. In Roger's apartment one year ago, after having had sexual relations, Ben cut his wrists in his only serious suicide attempt. Ben feels their relation had "lost its luster and beauty. It went into channels beyond comprehension. I felt there should be a bond between us. It meant nothing to him. I'd send him flowers. He'd be unappreciative." He explains that Roger had initially shown him "the finer things of life"—good dinners, shows, and so forth. After his suicide attempt Ben stopped seeing Roger for a while, but has now resumed the affair although on a less romantic basis.

Ben says he has grown weary of black men. When asked if Roger was white, he replied, "Yeah, he is a Jew. White men don't care what they do. They'll do anything. Negroes have limitations. If it lowers their pride, they won't do it. Things I won't do for no reason—too animal-like. Have to have emotional feeling or desire." Ben was vague and secretive about his relationship with Roger, at times attributing his secretiveness to shame over the "sordid" quality of the relationship and at times to a desire to prolong the interview sessions.

During his next visit Ben related the following dream:

> His nephew is in one room. Two men are in another doing something sexual. There is a door in between. He doesn't wish his nephew to see. He tries to close the door. His nephew struggles to open it. His nephew has a ferocious face. He swings his nephew around and knocks the head off one of the two men. He scrapes the skin of his nephew's face in doing this. It comes off as though it were a mask. He woke in fright.

Ben associates me with his nephew. He has seen me as wearing a mask. He has been considering the possibilities of an involvement with me much as he has been considering the possibility of an involvement with his nephew. He has become angry because he has not been given what he wants.* In the dream he is trying to conceal what went on between him and Roger.

He then revealed that his serious suicide attempt of a year ago came immediately after he had been induced to defecate on Roger. Although he slashed his wrists in shame and revulsion, he has repeated the experience with less guilt. He is still in conflict about whether he wants to stop this activity or not. He says, "I would like to get out of this filth but it's hard if you're up to your knees in it," yet his associations indicate that he has the wish to defecate on me.

In his last sessions he complained that no one gives him anything and that he is without desire or life—a reproach that was clearly directed at me. At the time of our last interview Ben was involved with the Baptist minister of his church. His message seemed to be that since I had not responded to him, he had found someone equally prohibited. He had asked the minister to "marry" him and then threatened to leave him to see how he would react. Although his wife now wants him back, he will not return to her, for he says that he is getting along better with her as things are now.

Knowing no father, Ben did not grow up with the picture of the violent male that Peter, Leroi, and Andrew received. However, his experience with maternal rejection and frustration appears to have been even worse than theirs, since in the early years of his life he had, in effect, no mother at all. Now he feels he is too demanding to be happy with anyone, male or female. Several times recently he felt like a baby and wished he could cry and ask his mother for understanding, although he was never able to lean on her or ask for help.

He is aware that he would like to be able to coerce affection. "I wanted my family to feel obligated to take

* His Rorschach responses pointed up his crude and intense dependency strivings ("yellow fat," "pieces of meat . . . raw meat") in the context of feelings of bodily disintegration ("two heads . . . looks like they're decaying").

care of me. I did this with Roger," he said. This was also his attitude toward me. He would call between interviews asking for help, advice, or medication, but always in a reproachful manner. He also harped on my lack of interest and eventual rejection of him.

His mother's affairs throughout his childhood served both to stimulate him sexually and to depress him emotionally. That so much of his homosexual activity is designed to come between men and women appears to derive from this source. An added factor in Ben's case pushing him toward homosexuality is his mother's strong preference for his sister and his envy of his sister as a consequence. When he has an affair with his sister's husband, he comes between the two of them, satisfies his envy, and punishes his mother and sister as well.

Both Benjamin Ellis and Andrew Vallen, in contrast to Peter Churney and Leroi Nifson, experience guilt, shame, humiliation, and degradation over their violent and destructive behavior and their homosexual activities.* It is worth noting that sexual activity for both consisted of their being penetrated anally. In Ben's case it is clear that he feels he deserves such abuse for his maliciousness.

Ben's greatest guilt and shame seem to derive from the things he has done to hurt or degrade others: turning his friend over to the draft board, sleeping with his sister's husband, setting fire to the apartment, and defecating on Roger. His suicide attempts appear in this context as gestures of atonement or penance. He now feels that he did not really want to die but did want people to think he genuinely hoped to end his life. On the other hand, he says there are things for which he cannot forgive himself and he admits he does not know when he might make

* Both received extremely high guilt ratings in the Hostility Inventory, in contrast to the first two men, who exhibited little guilt clinically and received strikingly low guilt ratings in their testing.

another attempt. His depression is great.

Ben, like Peter and Leroi, has his strongest involvement with a white man, Roger, who has shown him "the finer things of life." He makes a point of associating dirtiness with black homosexuals. While Ben would like to use his homosexual contacts to be cared for and protected, preferably by a white man, his need to degrade and be degraded is an equally important part of his racial preference. Both the need to be cared for and the need for degradation enter his fantasies with regard to me.

That four of the twelve male suicidal patients observed in this study were homosexual may not seem significant in so small a sample, but among hundreds of white suicidal patients the average is less than one homosexual in twelve patients attempting suicide. The possibility that the ratio of four in twelve is coincidental is 1 in 70 ($p = .014$). It should be kept in mind that since even comparative incidence figures concerning male homosexuality among the total white and black populations are not yet available, any definitive interpretation of the figures in the current sample is open to question.

Just as with suicide, variations in the dynamics of homosexuality from group to group are of even more interest than variations in rate. As with suicide, such information is important not just for what it reveals concerning homosexuality itself, but for what it reveals about the psychosocial pressures operating on everyone in a particular culture.

All three of the overt homosexual patients in this study are most attracted to white partners. This raises questions as to the prevalence and significance of the black homosexuals' preference for white men. To answer these questions and to explore further psychodynamic differences in the significance of homosexuality in the black compared with the white population, a separate study of black homosexuality is being undertaken. At present a detailed study of six additional black male homosexuals who are not suicidal has been completed. Four of those six also indicate a definite preference for white homosexual partners.

The idea that an anger-free, purifying whiteness could be incorporated or that blackness, which was seen as dirty and violent, could be obliterated runs through the Negro homosexual histories. Self-hatred directed at being Negro was, not surprisingly, strongest among the Negroes drawn to white males. Their sexual impulses and their black penises in particular were seen as alternately destructive and repulsive.

In only one of the ten homosexual cases had the father been totally out of the picture. Most often he was violent toward both his wife and son, so that the son was intimidated and rejected a male sexual identification, which he saw as requiring him to follow in his father's footsteps. The boys were often aware of and disturbed by their mothers' sexual activities with various men. They tended to see their mothers as unfaithful and promiscuous. The patients had themselves often had heterosexual experience—six of the ten having been potent in at least one such experience.* The violent father and the sexually unfaithful mother contrast with the typical families of white homosexuals, in which a passive non-violent father and a non-sexual mother are more common. Both the violence of the father and the

* While these figures may suggest that heterosexual potency is more frequent in the black homosexual than in the white homosexual, a much larger sampling of black homosexuals will be needed before any conclusion can be drawn.

infidelity of the mother were more prevalent among the homosexual subjects than among the suicidal subjects. With the suicidal subjects who were not homosexual the father tended to have abandoned the mother when the patient was a baby.

James Baldwin sensitively and powerfully explores the racial significance of suicide and male homosexuality in his novel *Another Country,* while at the same time indicating the importance of the white male to the black homosexual. Rufus, the black hero of the book, is filled with self-hatred because he hurts, degrades, and humiliates others through his sexual involvements with them, most significantly a white man and a white woman. The white woman is destroyed by his fury, although Eric, the white homosexual, is able to absorb it and emerge intact. Rufus' self-hatred is concentrated on his black penis, which he sees as a venom-producing weapon and ultimately as "his most despised part." In the months prior to killing himself his rage gets out of hand in his beatings of his girlfriend, his fights with strangers, and his threat to kill his best friend with a knife. He recalls his father's rage and, like so many of the subjects in this study, he stays away from his family for over a month prior to his suicide.

The night of his death, while taking the "A" train, presumably going back to Harlem and his family (throughout the book the Negro takes the "A" train to try to "make it" in the "other country") he fantasies the destruction and death of all the passengers. The train stops in Harlem and Rufus does not get off, realizing in that moment that he will never go home again. In jumping to his death from the George Washington Bridge he is aware of merging the blackness of his skin and of his life with the water below.

Throughout the book homosexuality is presented as a possible haven of tenderness from the frustration and destruction of living in general, and of heterosexual relations in particular. Rufus is doomed partly because homosexuality is not for him despite his earlier involvement with Eric, who replaces Rufus as the hero of the book. Relationships between the black and white male appear to have special redemptive power even for non-homosexuals. Vivaldo, Rufus' white friend, is guilty of not having loved Rufus sexually the night before he killed himself; he is convinced this would have saved Rufus' life. Eric, the white homosexual, is so glorified in the novel that sex with him—be it for Rufus, a black male, Cass, a white woman, or Vivaldo, a white male who redeems himself by having sex with Eric—seems to have almost magical significance.*

* In *Giovanni's Room,* Baldwin's other work dealing with homosexuality, the two main homosexuals in the story are both potent with women.

4

The Older Men

THERE is no more dramatic contrast to the younger patients, who were consciously struggling to control murderous impulses, than the group of suicidal black men who were over forty. They had curbed and repressed their anger in an obedient, submissive adaptation that had worked well for them since early childhood. When this adaptation failed them later in life they appeared to be without the emotional resources to do more with their frustration and rage than become self-destructive.

After drinking heavily to strengthen his resolve, forty-year-old Albert Mott jumped in front of a train in an attempt to end his life. Sideswiping him, the train badly cut his leg and side. In the hospital the following night Albert tried to jump out the window but was caught by one leg and pulled indoors.

Albert attributes his first suicide attempt to shame over the exposure of a sexual incident involving a nine-year-old girl whose aunt is his friend. Explaining that all the young girls in that home are fresh, sit on his lap, and rub against him, Albert says this girl started to fondle his penis, but stopped when she saw he had an erection and threatened to "tell on him." When she did, her aunt intended to call the police but was talked out of doing so by her boyfriend. Albert spent the night brooding about the incident, feeling ashamed that both the whole neighborhood and his two married sisters would know what happened.

Of his attempt in the hospital Albert says that he wanted to get everything over with and that he could not endure the pain caused by the injuries he received in jumping in front of the train. Nevertheless, a week later he did not want to die. "If you try twice and fail, what's the use?" he said. "It wasn't meant to be."

Albert had never married or lived with one woman for any length of time. He explains that women try to wrap you around their finger (as the little girl did in effect) and that he does not want this to happen to him. "If you are close to a woman and catch her in bed with another man, then what do you do? If you don't care about her, it won't bother you." He felt that all women cheat on a man and mainly want money, adding that without it you cannot have a woman. His closest involvement was with Janet, the nine-year-old's aunt. They had once been sexually involved but she now has another boyfriend and Albert visits her as a friend.

Albert says he can go for weeks without desiring a woman. "Once a month," he says, "I pay a woman for the night. It costs me an extra ten dollars since I always go the next day for a shot of penicillin to play safe." Denying that he has any particular interest in young girls, Albert stresses that the nine-year-old touched him and that he never touched her.

Emphasizing that he does not lead a wild life, Albert says he works all day and, if he goes out in the evening, comes home early and is in bed by eleven o'clock. Proud of having worked steadily since he was thirteen, Albert has been at the same firm moving clothes on a hand truck in the garment district for the past ten years. His take-home pay is only eighty dollars, yet he feels his biggest fault is not saving enough money.

Albert says he is athletic and works out in a gym several times a week to keep in shape. He likes boxing; he learned the sport while he was in the Navy, where he did some amateur fighting. Since he was thirteen, he has had few street fights; he has never started any but has won those he was in.

Albert tries to portray himself as "normal, average, the same as anyone else." He does not like the psychological tests, seeming to feel that having to take them implies abnormality. When asked about his dreams he says with some irritation, "I am perfectly sane." He clearly did not like questions about his family or his lack of closeness to them. He came close to losing his usual politeness when he warded off questions about his mother, saying, "How would I know? I mind my own business," a comment which conveyed quite clearly that he felt I did not.

Born in North Carolina, Albert never knew his father, who died when Albert was an infant. His two older sisters were put in an orphanage until he was three, when his mother went North and left her three children in the South with a friend, whom she paid for taking care of them. There they remained until Albert was nine, when they rejoined their mother.

Albert describes himself as an obedient child who was never in any trouble. In the tenth grade he left school for a CCC camp and at eighteen he went into the Navy, where he remained for nine years. He is proud of having been "the only Negro on the Admiral's barge" and comments, "You have to have a good record to hold that job." Albert does not like to discuss race problems, saying,

"You know about race in this country. If you do what you are supposed to do, no one bothers you." He feels his experience in the Navy was the best in his life because he traveled all over the world, had a good clean place to live, and felt secure financially. After his mother died when he was twenty-seven, he left the Navy and came to work in the New York garment district. He now lives in a rooming house; he rarely visits his sisters but calls on his old girlfriend and her boyfriend three times a week.

Albert has spent a good part of his life "doing what he was supposed to do." His attitude toward his work, toward the Navy, and toward race problems all indicate a compliant attitude toward authority. In obedience he has found security. Even his boxing is a controlled, regulated form of expressing any aggression he might feel.

His attempt to lead a controlled, regulated life, keeping his impulses under tight rein, results in a restricted and constricted emotional life. He lives alone and has no close friends and no real involvements with women.

All the experiences of which he is proud—the Navy, work, boxing—serve to reassure him about his masculinity while he retreats from a more primary masculine role with women. Much of this, including his involvement with a prepubescent girl and his explanation that "she did it first," has an adolescent quality.

He has only the most casual contacts with women, seeing them as exploitative, controlling, and unfaithful. He makes clear his view that if you do not care about women, they cannot bother you. His penicillin ritual after his once-a-month sexual contact has the quality of an attempt to ward off evil.

As a child he experienced maternal frustration like that of so many of the other patients. He appears to have wished to be away from his mother as soon as possible and stayed away from home until she died.* Despite his frustration and anger he has remained a "good boy." An emotional involvement with a woman would undoubtedly represent to him a frightening surrender of control.

When he succumbs to temptation with the young girl it is perhaps the first time his controlled adaptive system has so seriously failed him. He is unable to deal with the overwhelming shame and humiliation except by atonement—a view of suicide consistent with his overall attitude toward authority. While in the hospital he gradually realizes that no charges have been placed and the police are not after him. He begins to feel he can start life afresh in another neighborhood. Characteristically, he now feels he "wasn't supposed to die."

One night in his Manhattan apartment Jeremiah Pitts, a forty-year-old doctor, took fifty sleeping tablets. He had telephoned his girlfriend in Albany earlier in the evening and called her again after taking the pills. While he did not mention suicide to her, his thick, incoherent speech worried her enough to make her call a friend of his, who came to Jerry's apartment, found him unconscious, and took him to the hospital.

* His view of the world as reflected in psychological tests is one in which oral supplies are limited. Rorschach Card VIII: "fish bone, looks like a fish has been picked . . . like you've picked a crab." SCT, *I am afraid of:* "starving." On the Hostility Inventory he denies expression of anger or irritability—his scores here were among the lowest in the group. However, Rorschach percepts of "wild animals" and "wild plants" suggest that he is defending himself against potentially uncontrollable impulses. Recall his statement, page 73, during the interviewing that he doesn't lead a wild life, suggesting that his overt passivity represents a denial of unacceptable drives and impulses.

In discussing the causes of his suicide attempt Jerry claims that three major events led to it. Since he has been unable to work well recently, he has fallen into financial difficulty. He has also been disturbed by a shooting that occurred in his office six weeks ago. A robber entered his waiting room and told one of his patients and his nurse to lie on the floor. His patient resisted, reached for the robber's gun, and was shot and killed. After the killing Jerry was unable to work in the office and has been able to see patients only in the past two weeks. A third factor in his attempt was his relationship with his girlfriend Karen, a twenty-six-year-old divorced woman with two children. Jerry describes her as "the opposite of me, lackadaisical, someone who doesn't plan and takes things from day to day." In contrast he is fond of arranging things and gets upset if things do not go according to plan. They met two years ago and have been talking of her moving to New York, where she worked last summer. Since she has put off moving, Jerry visits her in Albany on weekends. She does not like to spend her weekends in New York because of her children. Jerry feels that Karen is warm, compassionate, and generous. He is sure of his feelings for her but says she is unwilling to remarry because her experience with her husband was bad.

Jerry initially listed as separate and disparate the three events that precipitated his suicide attempt. However, the psychological connection of financial problems, fear of violence, and difficulties with women became clear as the interviews progressed.

Jerry was born in New York just after his parents arrived from the South. Although they separated when he was eight, his father had a good job in a rubber company and always supported the family. Since he lived around the corner until Jerry was fifteen, they saw each other every day and often did things together. However, Jerry says, "My father was withdrawn. You couldn't talk to him."

Jerry describes his mother as domineering and inflexible. He lives near her and sees her three times a week, but he resents her continual advice. He says she may try to prevent Karen from visiting him, so that he won't be disturbed.

Jerry was perhaps closest to his grandmother, who lived with his mother intermittently from the time his parents separated until her death. He found her easier to talk to than either of his parents.

Unable to explain why his parents' marriage ended, Jerry says he never asked. They remained friends after their separation. Jerry describes both of them somewhat defensively as good parents.

Jerry says he was an obedient child who presented no problems. He never fought unless attacked, was an average student, and liked sports. He spent three and a half years in military service and won an athletic scholarship which paid for his college education. He used his G.I. bill to complete medical school.*

Ten years ago, over objections from his mother, Jerry married a woman he had known since high school. At the same time he accepted a job as a medical administrator in another state. He explains that his marriage broke up because of his wife's drinking, which increased after their daughter was born. He became angry, resenting having to do her work as well as his own, and then lost interest in her and wanted a divorce. After he obtained one he remained at his job for two years, but he became depressed because he was lonely and had little social

* Jerry's IQ was the highest of the group studied (115). Nevertheless, testing indicated that beneath a façade of competence and adequacy the patient actually felt extremely impotent, inadequate, and castrated. His difficulties with women include alternating views in which he is either the exploiter or being exploited. Having great difficulty integrating his own hostility, he showed responses suggestive of concern with concealment and disguise, as well as some suspicion. TAT stories suggested that he viewed death as a form of escape from unbearable tension arising from being neglected or alone.

life since there were only three black families in the community.

Becoming somewhat more open about himself, Jerry said his problem with Karen is the real issue in his life and he feels he has been hiding behind other problems. He has wanted Karen to marry him or at least to come to New York. Feeling that if she really cared for him she would come, he has suspected that there is another man in her life. He admits that he has no real basis for this suspicion. Jerry now thinks that if he had really wanted to die he would not have called Karen. He continued to discuss her throughout his interviews and expressed disappointment that her main concern over his attempt had been for what people will think of her.

He described Karen as inflexible and stubborn like his mother. While his mother is independent financially, Karen is not and he helps her with money. Jerry wondered if he were punishing Karen by not attending to his practice so that he has had less money to give her. Both his parents had encouraged him toward college and a profession. The fact that he thinks of punishing Karen, and perhaps his mother, by sabotaging his practice suggests that he sees his achievement as something done to please someone else.*

The tendency to punish himself to spite Karen came up during interviews which were continued while he was an outpatient. For example, if she did not want to come to New York for several days, he would tell her not to come at all and then feel hurt about it. He would then become depressed and lose interest in his work.

Jerry feels that both Karen and his mother "call the shots" in his relationship with them. His mother irritates

* His TAT story in response to the boy-violin scene is interesting in this regard. "Well, this little fellow knows he has to study his violin, but he'd rather be out playing. But he knows he's gonna have to study after all. Well, he's reconciled to the idea but he doesn't particularly care for it. That's it."

him by calling him three times every day, acting as though he were fragile and needed protection. He has never tried to stop his mother from treating him this way. In being dependent on his mother and his girlfriend while at the same time being critical of them, he resembles the earlier patients in this study. Yet he differs sharply from them in his avoidance of an open expression of anger. Nevertheless Karen claims to be afraid of him and gives as a reason for not seeing him her fear that he would harm her. Jerry feels this is only an excuse. Although she has made him angry enough to wish to throw things at her, he says, he has never actually done so. He makes great efforts to avoid being directly angry with her; when she is late he will look for reasons to justify her lateness. He says he is afraid of losing control. "If we had a fist fight or a violent argument, I could never again be friends with you," he adds. "I am slow to anger, but unforgiving if I get angry."

The psychological significance of his three initial complaints—difficulties with women, the dangers of violence, and financial problems—seems now to be clear. His frustrations with women, Karen and his mother, arouse the violent anger which he feels he must avoid. By curtailing his practice he punishes the women (and himself) without the need for any violent action.

While more intelligent and much better educated than Albert Mott, Jeremiah resembles him in wishing to lead a controlled, regulated life and in being upset if his arrangements do not go according to plan. Karen's more casual attitude probably attracts him, but it irritates and threatens him as well.

As we have seen, Jerry describes himself as an obedient child who never got into difficulty and never fought unless attacked. In his attitude toward school, work, and women he has felt obliged to behave as he ought rather than as he felt. As a consequence, like Albert, he presents a picture of emotional constriction. He does not appear to connect emotionally with Karen in a meaningful way. Nor does he seem to see himself or anyone else very clearly. His lack of interest in his parents' separation parallels a lack of interest in the reasons for his wife's drinking.

Behind his compliant façade his resentment was never hard to discern, although it was more masked toward Karen and me and more open toward his mother and his first wife. Under the stress of the relationship with Karen he appears to be close to losing the control he has tried so hard to maintain.

While in the hospital for treatment of his bleeding hemorrhoids, James Redler, sixty-eight years old, cut his wrists with a razor blade in an attempt to end his life. He did this at four o'clock in the morning and remained in bed bleeding until another patient awoke and called for a doctor. James says the impulse to kill himself was sudden and that he had not thought of it before going to bed.

James revealed all information reluctantly. He admitted to having been depressed for several months over financial troubles. While he had held the same job as a runner in a bonding firm for the last seven years, he owed his employer $250 and felt that he "bit off more than he could chew." What he meant by this became clearer when he revealed that he had given his life's savings, about $3,000, to his wife and children, who are now living in California, to enable them to make a down payment on a house. James has been sending them an additional $50 from his $264-a-month salary to help pay the mortgage. Even though he has had difficulty meeting the payments, he has not written his family about his trouble and, having no money for emergencies, was obliged to borrow from his employer.

James' wife had gone to California during the summers to visit their children and help care for their grandchildren. For the past six years she has remained there. He says that his wife and children want him to join them and that he would if he had enough money to make the move. But his explanation is not convincing. Although his wife appears to have made the decision to remain in California, the situation seems to suit James as well. He denies that this arrangement arose out of any difficulty with his wife, but there is clearly much in his relationship with her that he has withheld.*

James has always worked, been close to his family, and never had any major problems with drinking, gambling, or the law. He has had only two casual extramarital experiences since his wife has been in California. Despite his respectable life James very clearly feels that he is a failure. He went to a Negro college in the South for two years and regrets not finishing. He had left school thinking he would return but married instead. Convinced that his father and brothers achieved more than he, James mentions that his father owned his own house and that his brothers earn more money. In describing how he lost the family house in North Carolina, he became very sad.

* On the SCT, while he says that most marriages "last," he also states that after a year of marriage he "became dissatisfied." His conscious anxiety about heterosexual contact was also indicated on the SCT: *usually he felt that sex:* "was a secondary thing"; *when they talked about sex:* "I was a bit shy." The heterosexual scene on the TAT (Card 13MF) is viewed as a doctor and patient: "Could be grief over losing a patient. And he's turning to the table wondering what to do." On the Rorschach test, an unusual response was "a needle that takes blood," given to the vaginal area of Card VII and suggesting the feeling that sex may deplete one's strength.

After twenty years of ownership James was unable to meet the payments. It was at this point, nine years ago, that he and his wife came North. His children were all grown and were living in California, where his wife joined them three years later. James did not want to ask his children for help but will now accept his brother's assistance in getting to California, since the hospital decided to discharge him on condition that he join his family.

Of his father James says proudly that he worked at one job for fifty years. He was a janitor at a Southern university and did some private chauffeuring for university officials on the side. He describes his father as easy to get along with, able to care for his family's needs, and as someone who could both discipline his children when necessary and be kind to them in general. If he and the other children in the family "did wrong to the neighbors" or used bad language, they were spanked. Since they were all obedient, they were not whipped often.

The one dream James recalls involves both his father and his financial concerns. In the dream he is visiting his father (who in actuality died in North Carolina six years ago at the age of ninety-three) and his father is giving him money and advising him what to do with it.

James describes his mother, who died many years earlier, as a "good Christian woman." Although stricter and more outspoken than his father, she was kind and took care of them, he says. The oldest and most nervous of four children, James would hold back from groups and situations and had to be pushed into them by his mother. He feels he is like his father but less outgoing. He agrees that his wife seemed to make the major decisions in his own marriage.

"Hard-working" is the virtue James ascribes to himself and his father, "goodness" to his wife and his mother, and "obedience" to his siblings and his children.* The virtues of goodness and obedience, however, also describe his own behavior. He has lived his life doing what was expected of him without much regard for his own emotional needs or feelings. Most striking in comparison with the other patients, but linking him very much with Albert Mott and Jeremiah Pitts, is his description of himself as rarely becoming angry. Even in response to questioning, he could not recall a single instance of anger. Albert and Jeremiah also stressed obedience and hard work in describing themselves. Although he was polite and superficially compliant, James, like Albert and Jeremiah, was difficult to interview. The passive resistance that underlies their compliance seemed to bottle up all free emotional expression.

The emotional constriction that was part of his obedient adaptation appears to have prevented James, as well as Albert and Jeremiah, from meaningful emotional contacts, particularly with women. James expressed most emotion in discussing his father, whom he idealizes in a way calculated to help him maintain and reinforce his own compliance.

Despite a lifetime of hard work and obedience James finds himself at sixty-eight separated from his family and in debt. A sense of security, particularly financial, has been vital to him. A lifetime of effort seems to him

* On psychological tests, his drive for conformity and success was apparent throughout. On the Rorschach test, the number of "popular" responses was very high in relation to his total productivity. On the SCT, he indicates: *when he was completely on his own, he:* "was gentlemanly"; *he often wished he could:* "become president"; *he felt proud that he:* "was finishing high school"; and *I could hate a person who:* "didn't obey his parents."

James is functioning, according to the tests, at the "average" level of intelligence with an IQ of 96. In spite of his aspirations, intellectual and otherwise, he is quite immature socially and his ambitions may have exceeded his real potential, unlike those of others in this study who have much more undeveloped potential than they have been able to realize.

to have come to nothing. He resembles Jeremiah Pitts in the suddenness of the impulse to suicide after the collapse of a previously workable adaptation.

One morning while his wife was upstairs with several of their children, Edward Warner, fifty-seven years old, inflicted deep wounds with a razor on the right side of his neck. When his wife found him unconscious in the basement, lying in a pool of blood, she called an ambulance and Edward was admitted to surgery.

While insisting that he does not know why, Ed says he had been thinking of suicide for two weeks. Feeling that everything goes against him, he explained that, despite his job as a superintendent and his wife's work, they are unable to save money. Ed has never before tried to end his life and says he no longer wants to die. "I wouldn't want to go through that again," he explained. "It is not as easy to kill yourself as I thought."

Though he appeared somewhat tremulous, and admitted that alcoholism was a problem before his marriage two and a half years ago, he denied that it was a current problem or that he had been drinking in connection with his suicide attempt. It seemed doubtful that he was telling the truth.

Ed has no debts in New York but is troubled about owing $150 to an Alabama bank for about twelve years. His only arrest occurred four months ago when he was picked up for playing the numbers. He says he is not troubled by that incident, since the charges against him were dropped.

Denying any marital difficulty, Ed said that he had

not thought about arranging for his wife to find his body or about leaving her with five children, but he admits that it would have been hard on her. He remained evasive about the reasons for his suicide attempt throughout his first few sessions; he was also defensive in his attempts to deny that he had any emotional problems.

He was more willing to discuss his past history. The sixth of ten children, Ed was born and raised on a small farm in Alabama owned by his father. When he was nine, his mother died at forty-four of a stroke. He was with her at the time and says he can see it before him as if it happened only yesterday. His only other memories of her are of whippings that she gave him: once she beat him for throwing a stone at a pig and once for killing a chicken. "She was very strict," Ed explained.

After his mother's death his father raised the children. He describes his father as a normal, hard-working man who did not drink but worked and hunted. Ed followed him everywhere, felt he was closer to his father than any of the other children, and always obeyed and respected him. After the second grade Ed quit school to help his father raise cotton and potatoes on their farm. Once a year he still goes to visit his father and sister, who have remained there.

Ed describes himself as a good child who never fought or was in trouble. His earliest memory is of stealing watermelons with another child from land belonging to both their fathers. "If you stole from someone else and were caught they would kill you," he explains. In first discussing his father and his early years Ed did not mention his stepmother. He later revealed that his father had remarried right after his mother died. Describing his stepmother as domineering and as favoring her three children by a former marriage, Ed says he was disappointed that his father could not stand up to her more. At thirteen Ed left them and lived with an aunt until he went out on his own at seventeen.

When he was twenty-two he married a very attractive girl in his home county in Alabama. They were divorced within two years, "because she ran around with men and was no good."

Four or five years later Ed remarried and remained with his second wife for sixteen years. Throughout this marriage Ed says he drank, ran around with women, and spent whatever money he earned. He denies any strong dissatisfaction with his second wife except that she preferred working in the fields to keeping a clean house. They had no children together and Ed says he does not know why. Twelve years ago, he came North to get a better job. He found work as a handyman but his wife did not wish to leave her family and join him in New York. Since he was unwilling to return to the low wages of Alabama, they were divorced.

Ed had known his present wife, who is forty-two, for two years before going out with her. She had four children from a previous marriage, and they have had one child of their own since they married. He says she is a perfect woman: helpful, kind, and considerate. Ed makes a point of having "respected" his wife. They had sexual relations only once before they were married, and Ed comments, "If you mess around with women you lose respect for them."

Admitting that he has never loved any woman, Ed says he does not like to let anyone—man or woman—get too close to him. As a justification of his mistrust, he relates an instance when a friend of his told his present wife that he was running around with other women while courting her. She chose not to believe this. Ed says that he is very satisfied with his wife sexually and that he no longer runs around.

Describing his wife as very strict with her four older children, Ed says she spanked her twenty-year-old daughter as recently as one year ago. Nevertheless he feels their two-year-old son rules the house and that he can be firmer with him than his wife can. Ed admitted that he now drinks about ten beers a day and that he was having a mild case of DT's—he saw people dancing—at the time he began thinking of suicide.

When first interviewed, his wife supplied some vital information that Ed had suppressed. At the time of his suicide attempt they were scheduled to appear in court concerning a numbers charge against him. Two detectives had come to pick him up and were waiting in their car when Ed told his wife he was going to the basement to adjust the boiler, and cut his throat there instead. He had been brooding about the numbers charge since it was made four months ago. Ed talks of his never having been arrested before and of the injustice of his current situation. While he is sure he will go to jail, his wife thinks this is unlikely since they have never dealt in numbers and bet only occasionally.

Calm about discussing the details of his suicide attempt, his wife has a "live and let live" attitude about his problems. She sees neither his drinking nor their financial situation as problems, pointing out that he can afford a trip to the South each year. She says he is grown and must look out for himself, whereas she has five children to care for. She does not say this unkindly.

Although they seem to like and respect each other, theirs is clearly not a love marriage on either side. She is somewhat bothered by the fact that they are not legally married. She sees him as kind and openhearted with her and the children, and describes him as generally shy and quiet. She laughs when she says he has a little more nerve when he drinks, as though to say that she likes him better that way. She was aware of no evidence that he was depressed in the weeks before his attempt.

While Ed later confirmed his wife's story about his suicide attempt, he revealed that it is not really the numbers charge that bothers him but his belief that the police plan to use the charge as an excuse to turn him over to the Alabama police because of his $150 debt. He is sure he will be sent to jail in Alabama for two years and is terrified. "You know how they treat Negroes in Alabama jails since the civil rights movement." He thinks he heard the police say something about Alabama or turning him over but it gradually became clear that his idea is delusional.* He says he tried to repay the bank eight years ago but they would not accept his money on the grounds that his debt was a police matter. His wife feels this is just a "funny idea in his head" and doubts if he even owes money to the bank. In any case she is sure no one is after him. Ed appeared relieved to have his delusional ideas out in the open.

The possible sources of his need for punishment are worth exploring. In Ed's earliest memory, about stealing watermelons with another child from their fathers, he demonstrates an exaggerated idea of the consequences that would follow if he were caught stealing from someone else. Ed did not go on to steal from anyone else. Yet while he has worked hard and has never been in any difficulty with the police before, his delusion that he will be punished as a thief for not repaying a debt or for wanting to make money without work via the "numbers" suggests that he has probably had to make a great effort to repress acquisitive and larcenous impulses.

Any criminal inclinations that Ed may have would seem to stem from his relationship with his mother. His earliest memories are of severe beatings she gave him for throwing a stone at a pig and for killing a chicken. He

* In his constricted Rorschach record, Ed appeared severely disturbed, with very poor reality-testing ability and an inability to think along usual conventional lines. Some confusion and perseverative thinking were indicated, which were suggestive of possible organicity (brain damage). Marked regression, emotional insecurity, exaggerated needs for support, and impaired judgment were apparent throughout. His IQ was only 78 and his reading ability and range of information very limited. Some tests could not be administered because of this impairment.

sees her as strict and unloving. His stepmother's rejection of him and favoritism toward her own children only further heightened his mistrust of women. He says, "Women and cars are like cancers in your pocket, you never know when they will break down"—a remark that is particularly suggestive in the light of his witnessing as a child his mother's sudden death by a stroke.

Ed says he knows better than to love a woman because there are too many ways in which they cannot be trusted. He resembles the three previous patients in restricting his emotional involvements. His present wife, a strict Baptist, has given him no excuse to act out any dissatisfaction through relations with other women. This has probably only aggravated his sense of guilt. Ed has not legally married his wife and this may be a form of stealing from her or at least of not giving her what she deserves.

Ed identifies hard work and obedience with his early happy memories of his father. Like James Redler, he uses idealization of his father to reinforce his own compliance. Despite the delusional nature of his difficulties he resembles the three previous patients in the hard-working, non-violent, compliant adaptation that has characterized his life.

The breakdown of a submissive, compliant adaptation that had served to contain aggressive, antisocial impulses and the need for suicide as an atonement for the expression of such impulses gave these older black male patients a quality far different from that usually seen among older white male suicidal patients. These older black men see their adaptive failure in moral terms rather than in the terms of failure of achievement that more often characterizes the older white suicidal men.

The suicide attempts of these older black patients, with their emphasis on goodness and badness, have a rough similarity to the "moral" type of suicide seen in white suicidal patients who grew up in puritanical, religious backgrounds with an emphasis on obedience as opposed to self-expression, satisfaction, or pleasure. The white patients from this background, however, do not grow up into a society that insists on and reinforces the demands for obedience. When their adaptation fails them it usually does so by their early twenties. The black patients, particularly those from the South, grew up into a society that expected a continuation of an obedient, submissive adaptation into adult life. In some ways their childhoods were a preparation for what lay ahead. It is perhaps not surprising that one sees evidence of their adaptive failure at a later age. One senses that these older black men question whether a lifetime of attempting "to do the right thing" at the sacrifice of so much of themselves was worth it. Both the older black men and the younger white group see their adaptive failure in moral terms, as having been "bad" rather than "good." Whether they comply with or rebel against their environment, they have a strong sense of guilt and use suicide as a form of atonement.

It seems likely that these older, outwardly compliant black patients represent an adaptive pattern that is diminishing in frequency and that is primarily rural and Southern in origin. Certainly with the hard-working, never-in-trouble patient who proudly described his father as working for fifty years as a janitor and chauffeur at a Southern university, one feels that one is getting close to an adaptation that had its roots in the antebellum South.

In the case of the younger patients, conflicts with violent impulses did not seem to be significantly affected by whether their childhood was spent in the North or the South. While this may be an indication that Northern and Southern Negro adaptations are becoming more homogeneous, the qualification must be kept in mind that all the subjects are being studied while living under the stresses of an urban Northern environment and that black suicide as opposed to white suicide is primarily an urban problem.

5

Women and Suicide

MANY of the women described in the chapter on suicide and violence made suicide attempts in despair over being abandoned by a husband or boyfriend. In almost every case, it was clear that the current abandonment had opened up wounds received in childhood from an abandonment by the patient's mother.

The women in this chapter have suffered the same maternal abandonment. Yet their problems are focused more on pregnancy and motherhood than on abandonment by men. Maternal rejection in childhood has made them ambivalent about becoming mothers themselves. Growing up without fathers, or being forsaken by them early in life, contributed even further to an impaired conception of themselves as women and as mothers.

For many of these women suicide attempts were intimately connected with guilt about their pregnancies and subsequent rejection of their children. For the three patients described next, these conflicts were central, although the third did not actually bear children but interrupted her pregnancies with abortions. The cases demonstrate how the pressures on the black family are psychodynamically integrated by the woman so that they tend to be passed on to the next generation.

Before her suicide attempt Louise Greene, an attractive twenty-six-year-old woman who seems much younger because of her childlike manner, had written a note to an older boyfriend who was helping to support her. In her suicide note and during the interviews she insisted on her love for her children, yet in actuality she has rejected them. She has two children, a girl of seven and a boy of four, who live in the South with her relatives. She works as a waitress in a drugstore and sends part of her salary to help support them. She feels guilty about not having them with her and says she plans to bring them to New York this summer. In view of her life history her inability to care more for her children is not very surprising.

Louise was raised by her grandparents in Georgia. When she was twelve her mother, whom she had never met, appeared one day and told her that she now intended to live in Georgia and that she wanted Louise to live with her. Louise ran from the house and did not return until her grandparents came home from work.

Louise's mother wanted her to leave school and care for the many children she had had with various men. Her mother succeeded in taking her from her grandparents, but Louise frequently ran away from her to return to them. After a severe fight with her mother Louise was about to take rat poison when her aunt found her and prevented her from doing it. She does not accept the idea that her mother is really her mother, and although the man she has been told is her father is nice to her and says he is her father, she does not believe that he is.

While in Georgia, Louise had a child who has always

lived with Louise's aunt and uncle. At seventeen she went to North Carolina, where she had another child. She did not wish to marry the father of either; she said that the first had too many women and the second was too old and wanted to keep her at home.

Louise later married a man who was a year older than she. During the time she was married she kept her younger child with her. (This child, like the older one, is now living with her aunt and uncle.) She and her husband had numerous quarrels: he did not want her to work because the child was too young to be left with someone else. But Louise would not quit her job. "I don't let men tell me what to do," she says. Although Louise said she cared for her husband, she did not inquire very deeply into the circumstances of his death when, six months after their marriage, he was killed in a fight with another man. She says she had a nervous breakdown, could not sleep, and was under a doctor's care. When he talked of hospitalizing her, she became frightened and left for New York.

Louise also attributes her suicide attempt to "pains in her stomach." For three months she has had severe bleeding three times a month and looses a little blood every morning. Although she is very concerned about this, she does not know its cause and believes that "the doctors didn't tell me what is wrong. They treat me like some kind of kid."

Louise tolerates without pleasure whatever sexual intercourse she has with her boyfriend. She does not trust men, nor does she permit herself to be too close to them emotionally. Her not inquiring into the circumstances of her husband's death is striking in this regard. From her current boyfriend she is able to accept money but not much else.

Likewise, money is, unfortunately, the only thing she

seems able to give to her children. When living with her husband she did have her son with her, but even then her husband, although not the boy's father, seemed more concerned about his welfare than she did.

Louise feels too keenly her position as a rejected daughter to be able to see herself as a mother.* When asked about her current feelings toward her mother, she replies, "How should I feel toward her but cold? I was her first child—the only one she gave to my grandparents."

Her mother compounded Louise's resentment by coming back when Louise was twelve and demanding, in return for her years of neglect and rejection, total obeisance from her daughter, whom she wished to use as a maid and baby-sitter for her younger children. Being forced prematurely into the role of mother inevitably added to Louise's resentment of mothers and motherhood.

Louise reproaches her mother for having children with different men. Asked whether she had not done the same thing, Louise answered, "Not as many times. I don't want to be like her." But like her she is. Furious with her mother for abandoning her and for not providing her with a father, Louise is following in her mother's footsteps in having children with various fathers and then rejecting them. Like her mother, she has most rejected her first child—also a daughter. Louise goes from talking of her wish for "a new stomach" to an unconvincing intention of bringing up her children, whose education she is saving for. She seems to link her intrauterine bleeding with her rejection of her children—most likely as a punishment.

* The two themes of children and motherhood are referred to in a perseverative way on her SCT. She expresses great concern over her children, protesting that she wants them with her "forever," while critical of her own mother for having rejected her.

Barbara Weilen, thirty-four years old, blames her depression of several months and her suicide attempt with sleeping pills on the absence of her two youngest children, who were taken away from her two years ago and whose loss makes her feel lonely. Barbara does not now appear to be acutely suicidal but seems to use threats of suicide in a coercive way, saying in effect, "I don't want to kill myself if I can be sent away, get better, and then get my children back." Eventually it became clear that the loss of her children was related to her addiction to drugs and the problems this generated.

Barbara says her difficulties began with her mother's death when she was seventeen. Unmarried at the time, she delivered her first child in a pregnancy complicated by toxemia. As she was leaving the hospital she was told her mother had died. Her parents and twelve brothers and sisters had lived in a large three-story private house. After her mother's death Barbara returned there and, since she felt depressed and unable to cope with her daughter, gave the child to her married sister. Six months later Barbara married and she and her husband, Al, moved to their own apartment. During the next four or five years her daughter lived at times with her and at times with her sister. After their marriage Barbara and Al began to take drugs and had frequent and violent quarrels. Seven years ago, after a particularly vicious fight, Barbara left him, attempted suicide, and was then hospitalized for almost a year. Barbara also says that he is unreasonable and that their most recent separation occurred when he cursed her for not having food on the table when he came home. She cursed him back, shouting that dinner was ready and had only to be warmed. Angered by her words, he hit her. She told him to get out.

Despite his faults Barbara says that Al, a driver and delivery man for a soda company, is a good worker; he has been unemployed only for short layoff periods and has never stolen to buy drugs. In contrast she has stolen regularly over the last nine years to support her drug habit, has been arrested several times, and has had several short jail sentences. Barbara has also had "boyfriends" who gave her money for drugs. (Her brother claimed that she had been arrested for prostitution, but Barbara denied this.)

Two years ago Barbara and Al's four- and five-year-old sons were taken from her after she left them with her boyfriend, Harry, who in turn left them alone. Found by the police, one boy was placed in a state mental hospital and the other in a foster home. Barbara insists that neither of her children is disturbed and that they only need their mother. She protests the injustice of their being taken away. Barbara says she never got along with her daughter, who resents discipline and stays out late. She had always been afraid that her daughter would be raped and says her fears were realized when the girl was raped by six boys. "She is now in a Catholic school," Barbara commented, "and realizes I was right."

In her first sessions Barbara alternated between talking of missing her children and of missing Harry, whom she has known for five years and who has lived with her and her husband. Barbara says she loves Harry and they plan to marry, whereas her husband is more like a brother to her. "With Harry, I was happy," Barbara said. "He never fought me. He understood me. He'd throw something if angry or walk out of the house. He'd never hit me. I'd come after him and make up. I loved him more for that. He's away and my kids are away—nothing left." Harry has been in jail since shortly after the children were taken away. He was arrested for selling drugs and will be out in a few months. Barbara had a dream concerning him:

> Harry wished to come into her apartment and she would not let him in. Finally she does. They embrace and she tells him that even though she has not done anything while he was away, nevertheless she is up on some charges. Harry says he will help her get them dropped. They walk down the street with Harry holding her arm while she has her eyes closed.

Barbara related her reluctance to let him in to her resentment over what happened with the children she had left with him. In fact, she expresses little resentment toward him and concentrates it on the police and courts, etc. She does, in effect, have to close her eyes in order not to see Harry as he is. In her associations she also saw me as holding her arm and expressed the hope that I would give her active support in having her children returned to her.

When Barbara discussed her family she began by claiming that her mother showed no partiality among the children and then almost immediately contradicted this by saying that her two younger brothers and sisters came first. It was because of this, she feels, that she quit school when she was fourteen or fifteen to work as a domestic. She wanted money to buy her own clothes. Even earlier, however, she had been sent away to a youth home for playing hooky.

Barbara said her father would beat her for staying out of school, fighting with her sister, or being sassy or bad to her mother. Once, when he went to hit her with a strap, she jumped out of the window to escape. "He didn't know when to stop," Barbara said. "He's sixty-two and he will still take off his belt." Since her mother died, Barbara has come to know and like her father better.

When she was a child they were not close, partly because he was a fireman on an ocean liner and was away much of the time.

Barbara feels that as a child she was stubborn and always wanted to have her own way. She would stay out, go to parties and not come home on time, and had a very bad temper. Until she was sixteen or seventeen she fought frequently, most often beating up her older sister.

As one of twelve children, who felt that her mother preferred her younger siblings, Barbara experienced the maternal frustration of so many of the other patients in this study. She was determined from an early age to get for herself whatever she thought she did not get from her mother. She quit school to get money for the clothes that she felt her mother denied her. Her drug habit is perhaps best understood in this context. During one interview she persisted in asking for cigarettes until I got them for her. She commented, "I can't stand to be wanting anything."

Barbara's anger and violent temper originate as much in her experiences with her violent father as in her frustration with her mother. She has tended to mistrust and fight with men and is most accepting of Harry because he never hit her. During her present admission Barbara became violently angry because she was accused by several patients of always complaining. She proceeded to tell the whole ward to go to hell.*

Barbara did not like to see herself as a drug addict who has not been able to care for her children. Getting them back seemed to symbolize that she was well. Talking only of the idea of having them back, she never spoke of the children as individuals or used their names. The

* Her unusually high score on the Hostility Inventory suggested that she is in an almost constant state of anger and irritability. Her assaultive behavior is easily triggered by the environment.

same was true of Louise Greene, the previous patient, who also never referred to the personalities or names of her children.

For both Barbara and Louise Greene the subject of their mothers elicited strong emotion: anger for Louise, guilt for Barbara. Barbara's situation was complicated by her mother's death while Barbara was delivering her first child. That she viewed her pregnancy as responsible for her mother's death was not surprising, since her being pregnant was part of the acting out of the angry defiance of her mother that characterized her adolescent years.* Her feelings toward her mother were delineated by guilt, anger, and frustration—all of which contributed to her ability to give even less to her children than she felt her mother gave to her.

Willa Marsh, a very dark woman of thirty-four, jumped out of a fourth-floor window and fractured her cervical spine in an attempt to end her life. In the throes of an acute psychotic episode that had begun a week before her admission to the hospital, Willa gave dramatic expression to her conflicts in her delusional ideas.

For about a week before her attempt she suspected that "they" were out to get her. She felt that people looked at her strangely on the street, laughed at her, and talked about her. Similarly, Willa believed that actors on radio and television talked to her and about her. They conveyed the idea that she was to have her genitals mutilated or that the police would arrest her. At times

* SCT emphasized her sadness and guilt over her mother's death.

"they" became other nations or the whole world. When she jumped from the window in her most recent attempt, no voice spoke to her, but she had become so frightened she wanted to hide. In telling her story, Willa wondered occasionally if everything had taken place only in her mind.

For some time Willa has known she has uterine polyps. She had been told that she should be re-examined within the next month and that she would eventually need a hysterectomy. During her menstrual periods she has such severe pain and such large clots that she says she sometimes has difficulty in telling whether she is menstruating or having a miscarriage. Since doctors are involved in her fear of being genitally harmed, she worried about what she should tell me and felt that she may have told too much, saying she does not wish "to say anything bad about the doctors."

A week before her suicide attempt, about the same time she began to feel persecuted, she was fired for frequent absences from her job in a bookbindery where she had been working for three years. Willa explains that she would stay out drinking and adds that she would stay home a few days if someone hurt her feelings. "If I'm teased I'm hurt and that's not right since I like to tease people myself."

After losing her job she became upset, began drinking more, and became more upset when she tried unsuccessfully to reach her boyfriend. For several days he was not home and did not call her. Since she was afraid of being alone, she spent the rest of the week with Paul, an old boyfriend. When they were at the house of a neighbor who had a young baby, she talked of suicide and impulsively jumped out the window after telling her hostess to take care of the baby.

Born and raised in South Carolina, Willa never knew her father. For some time he had been in and out of jail until, while her mother was pregnant with her, he killed someone and was imprisoned for life. Her mother never spoke of him. After giving her three children to an aunt and uncle whose children were already grown, Willa's mother went off to live and work in town. As a child Willa felt that her aunt preferred her sister, with whom Willa frequently fought. Now she feels her aunt "just didn't have any time for me," adding, "I realize it's hard to have a child." Willa would often stay out at night and was frequently whipped for this. Her sister and brother were more obedient.

When Willa was eleven her aunt became upset because her husband was running around with other women. "My aunt took a gun and shot herself in the womb right in front of me," she recalls. Willa ran from the room in terror but returned when her aunt called her back to remove her shoes while she lay bleeding. Although her aunt survived and lived many years, Willa's eyes filled with tears when she said that their relationship contributed to the mess she has made of her life.

In the weeks after she shot herself Willa's aunt became furious because Willa wept so often and eventually sent her back to live with her mother. She had her first sexual experience when she was fourteen and, fearing she had become pregnant (she had not), she drank turpentine in a suicide attempt or gesture. As she explained, "Everyone [her mother] in the South was saying don't get pregnant and don't come back here if you do."

Willa came North when she was seventeen. Despite her difficulties she has worked regularly in bookbinderies during her seventeen years here. For ten of those years she was involved with Paul, who, she says, eventually tired of her.

Willa's conflict over pregnancy and childbearing runs throughout the interviews.* The first thing she says of

* These themes were also reflected in the psychological tests. On the SCT (administered orally since she said, "I can't read that good"), the patient indicated: *Most of all I want:* "a baby." To

her brother and sister is that her sister has "lots of kids" and that her brother has "one kid." Willa says she has seen all her friends have children and wishes she could too. She takes no precautions with her current boyfriend, George, and has been hoping she will become pregnant. Nevertheless, earlier in their relationship, when her period was late, she took medicines to bring it on. While thinking that she can become or may be pregnant reassures her of her womanliness, she is terrified at the prospect of actually having a child.

Willa has always feared pregnancy, explaining that she cannot afford to stop work and that "a man always leaves you when you have children." Relating this to her father's "leaving" when her mother was pregnant with her and her mother's inability to manage, she adds that men do not want the responsibilities of providing for a child. When two or three times she thought that Paul had made her pregnant, she took medicines to induce bleeding and feels guilty because of this. She appears to have learned from her aunt to "attack" her womb as a way of dealing with fears of abandonment by a man. Willa expects to be punished for "not being productive, for not having children," and for her sexual behavior in general. Willa is in an impossible bind: she feels damned if she does have a child (her man will desert her) and damned if she does not (she is not really a woman, is not productive, etc.).

Willa feels guilty for flirting with other women's husbands, for letting men take advantage of her because she

---

the TAT picture of a girl leaning over a bridge (Card 17GF), she told a story that was suggestive of a psychosis in its inappropriate introduction of the virgin-birth theme. Verbalizing a strong belief in Christ, she experiences guilt in relation to her hostile impulses, which may be directed, in particular, toward children or siblings: *She felt she had done wrong when she:* "spanked her baby"; *I feel guilty about:* "the baby falling"; *She felt she could murder a woman who:* "beats her children," etc. With an IQ of 74, the patient showed few, if any, resources, with a defective ability to test reality appropriately.

is lonely, and for interfering with pregnancy. She sees the hysterectomy as a genital punishment she deserves for genital crimes. At the same time she has strong anxieties about her sexual identity. She thinks the turpentine she took at fourteen ruined her insides and worries that the catheter that was used in the hospital did something that would prevent her from being a woman. She is afraid that in the operation "the doctors will fix" her so that she "is unable to be a man or a woman." Willa's fear of pregnancy (recall her mother's words, "Don't get pregnant and don't come back here if you do!"), her fear of rejection by her man, and her pervasive feelings of guilt combine to immobilize her. It is not surprising that she is afraid an operation will make her a neuter, since this would give concrete expression to how she already feels.

Her anxieties over George's diminished interest in her, the loss of her job, and the prospect of a hysterectomy all converged to produce an acute psychosis. By the end of a month in the hospital Willa presented a different picture. Her psychotic ideas appeared to her like an old dream. She had arranged to get her job back and she felt she wanted to eat, work, be healthy, and not let anything bother her. Early in her sessions Willa had said she regarded suicide as a crime for which one went to hell and was not forgiven. Toward the end of her stay in the hospital she was cheerful, coherent, and clear about her desire to live.

The attitude expressed by Willa that "a man always leaves you when you have children" was expressed by a high percentage of the black women in this study. Most of their mothers had been abandoned by their men before or shortly after a child was born. A fearful equation between pregnancy and abandonment was inevitably a far more frequent occurrence than one sees in a comparable group of white women. The women's resentment toward their children usually reflected their resentment toward the men who deserted them.

Self-hatred that is tied to failure to raise one's own child is certainly seen as an important motivation among white suicidal women. However, for the black woman, a history of childhood rejection followed later in life by abandonment by the father of her child is so much more common than among whites that it is not surprising that it plays an even more important role in the suicide of young black women. It probably contributes to the fact that among young adult black women as well as young black men, the urban suicide rate is higher than among their white counterparts.

The following women were also faced with conflicts concerning illegitimate children, but their stories are quite different. While both women suffered a good deal of frustration in their relationships with their mothers, they are among the few subjects in this study who could and did turn to their fathers for emotional sustenance. The over-intense attachment of both women to their fathers interfered with their relationships with men. An acute reaction to rejection or abandonment by their fathers was decisive in their becoming pregnant. However, the very importance of these fathers in their lives contributes to making these two women more closely resemble white female suicides than the other black women in this study.

Marjorie Allen, an attractive twenty-year-old woman, explained her suicide attempt with sleeping pills by saying that things had been getting her down for several months, and for the past three weeks she suspected that she was pregnant. Although she had not yet had any pregnancy tests, Marjorie's period was over three weeks late and she did eventually prove to be pregnant. Her boyfriend Larry, a twenty-four-year-old bandleader, wants them to marry, but Marjorie, who has known him for four months, is unsure whether she wants to marry him.

Three or four months before coming to New York from Washington, Marjorie had moved out of her parents' house after a fight with her father. He had objected to a previous boyfriend, Alan, who had a prison record. Several months later, when Marjorie wanted to end her relationship with Alan, she moved to New York. She spoke of being too proud to go back to her parents' home, and said her father was too proud to admit he had been wrong. Marjorie has felt depressed about the fight with her father and much of her reaction to her pregnancy involves concern over how he will react.

Marjorie says that her mother likes to stay home and watch TV and to go to church on Sundays, but does not enjoy visiting. She describes her father as more sociable and adds that, in her family, "we had most anything we wanted."* Marjorie and her father got along well and went on trips together. Although she feels her father drank a little too much, "like most fathers," he worked steadily as a cook in a hospital in Washington. She says proudly, "He is a good cook." When she was between eight and ten her father was sick (probably with tubercu-

* Psychological testing suggested that, at least in fantasy, Marjorie sees her life with her parents as one of personal security and satisfaction. To the family farm scene of the TAT (which usually elicits stories about a girl going off to school), the patient tells a story of family togetherness, ending, ". . . after the day is over, they sit around the table and have their supper and then sit up for a while and talk, then go to bed and think about what they do the next day. That's about all." While the male is viewed as irresponsible and weak, he is forgiven and looked to for support and nurturance. Both her rage and dependency are on a very primitive level. Strong underlying castration feelings and a sense of bodily damage and incompleteness are indicated.

losis) and away from home. Since her father's illness her mother has had to work as a domestic.

Marjorie has a nineteen-year-old brother who is a freshman in a Negro college. Like her mother, he prefers to stay home and read. He never went out much in high school, while Marjorie, who feels she is more sociable like her father, went out all the time. Whereas her brother was her mother's favorite, she was her father's. Marjorie recalled that her brother would protest when she got things from her father that he did not get. She said that if her father would also get them for her brother, she would become very angry and tear up her room. If her father made her obey her mother she had a similar reaction. "After a while I got tired of putting the room together again and I stopped," Marjorie said.

In discussing her childhood Marjorie said she was a tomboy and has been told by her mother that she never cried. She was in frequent fist fights defending her brother, until the end of elementary school; although she was only a year older she was much bigger than he. Asked if she ever hit him, she recalls that she had once tried to beat him but her father stepped in and broke up the fight.

In discussing her relations with boys, Marjorie said she had been too busy being "evil" to be nice to them. She will not sit and talk to them and, if she does, she may holler or scream at them. She thinks a boy who gets excited about her is a little crazy and says she likes a man to be interested but not too excited.

In describing her relationship with Alan, the ex-convict she left Washington to avoid, Marjorie explained that she did not know of his criminal record until two months after meeting him. When her father ordered her out of the house, he had been drinking. Marjorie says she knew she did not really have to leave. She punished both him and herself by moving in with Alan and regrets her involvement with him; she insists that she would not have gone to live with him if her father had not told her to leave.

Marjorie was deeply moved by my raising the question whether her pregnancy and suicide attempt were intended to hurt her family through hurting herself. Much of her behavior seemed to have this character—even her breaking up her room in anger as a young girl.

During the course of the interviews Marjorie reported the following dream:

> Her grandfather wished her to take a trip with him. She said she could not.

Marjorie said her grandfather had died four years ago. "He was like a father to me," she explained. She had once, at fourteen or fifteen, run away to his place in another state when she did not want to go to school. She is a Baptist and hopes to meet her grandfather again in an afterlife.

In discussing her dream Marjorie said she felt her grandfather is really referring to death in suggesting a "trip." She seems to be attempting to reject or disengage herself from union with her father or grandfather in life or death. Marjorie then began to talk of her fears of death, which were particularly strong when she was eight or nine. Just after her father's mother died, she was afraid that she herself would be with "the devil" because she so frequently pushed her brother down the stairs. She spoke of her terrible temper and said she would lock her mother out when her mother left the house.

Although Marjorie and her father have made up and he has invited her to come home, she feels she cannot because she is going to typing school and likes her job in New York. She spent a day visiting friends and family with her father and she came in talking of how lively and full of fun her father was. She says her current boyfriend, Larry, is very much like him, but she stresses her indifference to him, saying, "I don't let a boy mean too much. I am afraid to be involved."

At the time of Marjorie's final interview she was considering marrying Larry. She now knew definitely that she was pregnant and had decided to keep the baby. She had spoken to her mother and father on the telephone and they accepted the idea.

Marjorie reported the following dream:

> Her cousin's baby was with her cousin's mother. Her cousin's mother liked the baby so much that she wanted to see the cousin again.

She explained that her cousin and her mother have quarreled and do not see each other. Although the baby was initially related to her fantasies about her father, her present hope seems to be that through renouncing union with her father, and presenting her mother with the baby, she will reach some equilibrium.

Unlike so many of the mothers of the other patients, Marjorie's mother had raised her daughter. Yet Marjorie harbors a good deal of resentment and bitterness over her mother's emotional withdrawal from her and her preference for her brother. Marjorie's mother withdrew from her husband as well and seems to have little conception of herself as a wife to her husband.

Her mother's withdrawal permitted Marjorie to become her father's companion and allowed them to become important to each other in a manner that carried overtones of more than father-daughter closeness and that was bound eventually to present both of them with problems. In a sequence of associations that went from pushing her brother down the stairs to locking her mother out of the house, Marjorie made clear her anger toward both of them as well as her desire to have her father to herself. Having become her father's companion, Marjorie's sensitivity to abandonment by him was acutely developed in the two years he was away from home because of his serious illness. Her fears of death after her father's mother died occurred during this same two-year period. It seems plausible that Marjorie had wished it was her mother and not her father who had "gone away."

Her father's overreaction to her relationship with Alan suggests that he was also having difficulty in handling the feelings stirred up by his relationship to Marjorie. She then reacted with the need to punish him in an expiatory way, which would hopefully lead to reconciliation. Both her pregnancy and her suicide attempt seem reflections of this wish.

Marjorie's somewhat neurotic involvement with her father appeared to be preventing her from allowing any other man to mean very much to her. Her suicide attempt has contributed to making her aware of the self-destructive nature of this involvement. As of my last interview with her, however, she was not contemplating permitting another man to replace her father in importance, but rather intended to adopt her mother's diminished conception of the role of a wife. In keeping her baby and marrying Larry without too much involvement with him, she would appear to be following in her mother's footsteps.

Three or four days before her suicide attempt with twenty tranquilizers, Jean Wayne, a young girl of eighteen, says that her boyfriend Jimmy told her that they should stop seeing each other. Although she said she had no idea anything was wrong, she admits when questioned that he had not called or seen her much during the two weeks that preceded his wish to end the relationship. Jean said that this is the third time a boy has left her and that she felt she could not take it any more.

Jean met her first boyfriend, Ollie, shortly after her father died when she was thirteen. She says she took her father's death very "hard." Feeling abandoned and worthless, she tried to replace him by becoming sexually involved with Ollie when she was fourteen and he was seventeen. She became pregnant at fifteen, about the time Ollie left for the service. When she next saw him, he was married and had children. Jean's child, a girl, now lives with a childless married cousin. Although she talks at times of taking the child back after she finishes high school, she does not really seem to want this. Later becoming involved for six months with a young man named Bo, Jean considered suicide when he left her for another woman but decided against it.

Although Jean's parents were from Alabama, they met in New York. Jean, their only child, was born and raised in New York City. Her father was employed as a carpenter until his bad heart prevented him from working; he died a year later. Jean says he was very nice to her when she was little, brought her things, and took her places. In his last years he would drink and become abusive, occasionally hitting Jean and her mother. When questioned about his behavior she defended him, saying that I had to understand that he was ill.*

* A strong tie to the father with possible Oedipal implications along with sensitivity to rejection by the male was reflected throughout the TAT stories. A masculine, phallic component in her own behavior may play a role in the events leading to her being rejected. On the TAT, she dealt with suicide themes, as a consequence of the girl being rejected by a man. On the SCT, however, she indicates: *A person who falls in love:* "is crazy"; *Love is:* "there's no such thing as love." While expressing shame over her attempt to kill herself, she also showed a preoccupation with violence. With an IQ of 92, her range of information is extremely limited (she says that "rubber comes from an animal, I know, but I can't recall"; and thinks that Brazil is in Europe). On the Rorschach test, her thinking was revealed to be quite idiosyn-

Before meeting her mother Jean's father had left his first wife and their two children to live with another woman. By the time he left that woman, she too had two children. Jean became tearful when she revealed that he had never married her mother. She feels hurt about his failure to marry her and does not accept his explanation—that his wife would not give him a divorce—since she thinks he could have obtained one if he had really wanted to. Dreaming frequently of her father, Jean imagines him in the hospital or doing carpentry at home. She spends time wishing that he were alive. She has been told she would not have had a child if he had lived, but she does not know if this is true. Becoming upset and tearful whenever the loss of her father or boyfriends comes up, Jean stresses her feelings that men are unfaithful and feels that she never wins out if there is another woman.

Since Jean was five her mother has worked as a seamstress in a factory. There have been no men in her life since her husband died. She has been critical of Jean's schoolwork and her boyfriends, yet Jean describes her as "quiet, shy, similar to me." There seems to have been little closeness between them.

Revealing that she generally feels people have treated her unfairly, Jean says she failed history this year because her teacher was unjust and she was worried about graduating from high school on time. Similarly, she thinks that other people—at school, in the hospital, and at her part-time job—treat her unfairly. As evidence, she said her employer only cared about when she would be coming back to work. "He didn't care how I am." She was resentful of all the testing and interviewing she underwent in the hospital, regarding this as an unfair imposition.

---

cratic and possibly autistic, overly concerned with bodily functioning and somatic concerns that arise from an internalization of her hostility.

When seen as an outpatient, Jean seemed more cheerful, felt thankful she was alive, and was sure she would never again attempt suicide. She had seen Jimmy for an hour and commented that he said they would see each other but less frequently than before. She did not press him to find out why he did not want to resume their relationship—evidently because she did not want to face hearing of another woman.

She had one dream the night after she had spoken to Jimmy:

> There was a shoe sale. There was nothing her size. Everything was too small.

Fond of buying shoes, Jean explained that she loved to do this after she gets paid. She then talked of her hour with Jimmy. It is clear that she feels what he offers her is too little and certainly no bargain.

Jean concluded her last visit by discussing her pregnancy, her child, and her plans for the future. She feels it is probably better for all concerned if her child stays with her cousin as long as the cousin does not return to work. She now hopes to finish high school in June and then to get a full-time job. She has been majoring in accounting.

Jean intends to live at home until she is twenty-one because she feels she will need her mother if she gets into trouble. She says she does not wish to marry until she is twenty-four or twenty-five, explaining, "I'd like to have a good time before marriage." Asked if she thought that good times end with marriage, she replied that she thinks this is so and that one marries just to have a family and children.

Jean's ambivalent attachment to her father, whom she sees as later having abused and rejected her, plays a decisive role in her relations with men and in her suicide attempt. Both her father's refusal to marry her mother and his death are seen as rejections of her. His death appears to have precipitated her early pregnancy and also seems to have made her particularly sensitive to the rejections by men that followed. Marjorie Allen held on to her father by trying not to care too much about other men. Jean, whose father is dead, seems to try to replace him by caring too much too quickly regardless of whether the man warrants her interest or affection. Nevertheless, there are indications that she holds on to her father by unconsciously seeking both the attachment and the rejection with other men that she experienced with him.

Her parents, like Marjorie Allen's, do not appear to have been close. Her mother's attitude toward her is predominantly critical. Like Marjorie, who has similarly been frustrated by her mother, Jean can only visualize giving up her attachment to her father by becoming more dependent on her mother.

Histories of neurotic attachments to the father in families where the mother and father are not close; consequent interference with their ability to form satisfactory relationships with other men; extreme sensitivity to rejection, death, or abandonment by the father or other men—all are a familiar story to anyone working with the problem of female suicide in the white population. Such a history is far less frequent among black women because the father is so seldom available for this sort of relationship.

In their unresolved Oedipal problems with their fathers, Jean and Marjorie present a pattern more typical of white female suicides than those of any of the other patients in this study.

Unlike the two previous patients, who came from relatively stable families, Gloria Taylor not only did not have a stable family, she could be said to have had no family at all. Raised in a series of foster homes where obedience was the price she had to pay for care, Gloria was not able to afford the luxury of anger. That she survived at all is a credit to her spirit; the emotional constriction she developed in the process would seem to have been impossible to avoid.

Gloria is a twenty-two-year-old medium-brown woman who made a suicide attempt with sleeping pills on New Year's Day following a break-up with her boyfriend, Lonny. On New Year's Eve he came to see her and said he wanted to go to several parties alone and would return after midnight. She rejected his plans for her and told him that they had better end things between them. Lonny had disappointed her in a similar way on Thanksgiving and Christmas Day. That evening she went out with some friends but was depressed. When she awoke the next day she felt intense pain, kept thinking that she lost out in whatever she wanted, and decided to end her life.

Gloria had known Lonny for five months and had seen him exclusively for the past three months. She made a point of saying that their relationship was more than sexual. Later it emerged that she had had sexual relations with him only once and refused him subsequently because she did not enjoy it. Neither of them could express affection easily.

Gloria admits that she may have a sexual problem. When she has sexual dreams she often wakes with a pain in her vagina. When questioned she says she has no homosexual history and never masturbates, commenting that she is shocked at the idea of either.

Gloria's other serious relationship with a man took place when she was eighteen and ended mainly because of her sexual fears. A year ago, partly to try to overcome these fears, she had sexual relations with a man she had just met. "We were together only twice and I became pregnant," she says. When this man learned that she was pregnant, he told her that he was married and had his own children. He did not help her with her subsequent abortion.

Unable to recall the first three or four years of her life, Gloria does not know who cared for her. In her earliest memories she is with her first foster parents in Albany. She was brought to them at four and remained with them until she was ten. Neither of her foster parents was physically affectionate. Her foster mother was particularly unkind and beat her frequently with a broomstick. Fearing her, Gloria would often sleep on the porch rather than come into the house. She feels that the families that took her wanted her only for the money they received for her care.

When Gloria was about six her foster father abandoned the family after an argument with his wife. Gloria was sent to bring him back and remembers calling after him as he walked away from her. They never saw him again.

When she was eleven, Gloria was placed with a family that had had seventeen children of its own: ten grown and out of the house and seven that had died. There were three other adopted children living in the house. Gloria said she felt like a stranger at first but was happy there after a while and says her twelfth year was the best in her life.

When she was fourteen her happiness was spoiled by a seventeen-year-old boy who raped her when he was drunk. He had followed her home and attacked her outside her door. Afraid her foster mother would be angry, she was unable to call for help. Although the boy received a sentence of three years, people said she had "led him on." "They put me down for it and rubbed my nose in it," she said. When she described the scene in detail, it sounded as though she had been raped as a consequence of not being emotionally able to defend herself. Her foster mother told her she could no longer stay with them if she were pregnant. "Fortunately, I was not," Gloria says.

When she had difficulties in school, Gloria was sent to a school for retarded children. At seventeen she finished school and worked as a wrapper. She came to New York from Albany soon after because her mother had written to her and asked her to come. Until then she had never met her mother. She and her mother, who was then forty, were together for three months. Gloria said her mother's drinking and her thirty-year-old husband's advances prevented her from getting along with them. She moved into a rooming house where she lives alone without any real friends. She feels you can keep friends only if you do not bother them too much. She often reads in the library when not seeing her boyfriend or working in the old-age home where she is a nurse's aide.

Although Gloria says she cannot talk to women as well as to men, she arouses a very maternal reaction from the nurses on the ward. Her helpless appearance reaches out and invites protection. After she was discharged from the hospital one of the nurses took her home for a while. Similarly, Lonny's mother visited her in the hospital and took her home when Lonny was away.

When seen as an outpatient Gloria was apologetic about everything from reading books in the waiting room to asking a question. She says she is this way because she is afraid to make anyone angry. She makes the point that although she "bends over backwards" to do things for people, she loses all her friends. "It must be something in me," she says. It is only in the area of sex that she refuses to be ingratiating. In the light of her sexual history this is not too surprising.

Gloria speaks deliberately, seriously, philosophically, and circumstantially. Her thinking is also very concrete.* She is able to recall the exact dates that things happened to her: she was raped on December 24, she broke up with her first boyfriend on February 28, etc. She would question and test me to see if I understood her. When I forgot a minor detail in her story, she was reproachful.

Gloria stressed her honesty. "I won't lie. I'll tell you if I don't wish to answer." She spoke of her mistrust of people and told of a girlfriend who had used her confidences against her. She seemed to fear that I would do the same. Although she stressed her mistrust, she gave the impression of being childlike, open, and defenseless.

She told of a dream in which she was believing a patently false story of Lonny's and then went on to lose him to a faceless girl. She felt that her inability to protect herself in the dream reflected her actual situation.

As her sessions went on Gloria felt more and more that her suicide attempt was an attempt to punish Lonny. She feels she becomes part of someone and cannot tolerate losing him.

Gloria often dreams of death. She related a dream of four years ago that impressed her. She dreamed of a woman in a coffin with her arms moving. Gloria saw a nickel on the floor and picked it up. This seemed to relate to her feelings toward her foster mother and her

* Her IQ in testing is at the borderline level of functioning (77), with strengths which suggested that she might be able to appear much better integrated and possibly more intelligent than she actually is. On the Rorschach test her reality-testing ability was revealed to be highly variable. On the SCT and TAT she clearly implied that she sets standards for and expectations from others and then is often disillusioned by people. Nevertheless, she appears to deny becoming angry at them. Death is viewed as an event which elicits remorse from others. She appeared to feel keenly her lack of education and she fantasies goals which under the circumstances are clearly unrealistic for her.

attitude that money meant more to her than Gloria did. She seemed to be saying in return, "I wouldn't give a nickel for your life."

The saddest thing about Gloria's life is the totality of her emotional constriction. She lives alone with no close friends. Sexual and emotional involvements with boys are painful for her. Useful anger or self-assertion are impossible for her.* She related a dream in which she said, "I had a cancer inside me," which seemed to express the destructive effects of the internalization of her anger. She has frequent dreams in which she sees herself as dead in a casket—an accurate reflection of the life she is living. Even her job in an old-age home seems to be part of this pattern.

Gloria, unlike most of the young patients in this study, is no danger to anyone but herself. In the total impounding of her rage, her emotional constriction, and her need to be a good girl, she is quite similar to the older men who have been discussed—that is, she reflects an adaptation that is seen less and less frequently among the black population, particularly among the young.

Although Louise, Barbara, and Willa had mothers and fathers who did not care for them, and Marjorie and Jean found consolation only in their fathers, while Gloria

* While she received a fairly high rating on the Hostility Inventory, this is despite the fact that she is the only patient to receive an absolute 0 in the assaultive behavior factor of that scale—a pattern which suggests the necessity she felt through life to avoid showing her anger. Her low rating for negativism is consistent with this. It is high ratings in suspicion, irritability, and guilt that give her a relatively high total score.

could be said to have had no parents at all, all of these women have arrived at maturity without reaching a sense of themselves as women. Having been abandoned, exploited, rejected, or forced into a premature independence by their mothers and fathers, these girls inevitably disparage themselves while viewing men with mistrust. Their subsequent experiences with men only hardened this mistrust.

All of the women in this chapter have at one time or another been made pregnant and abandoned. Most of the pregnancies took place when they were girls of sixteen or seventeen. These early sexual experiences and pregnancies were usually motivated by a self-damaging defiance of frustrating parental figures. Being unable to function as mothers further damages their ability to see themselves as women and interferes with their capacity to enjoy men. As a consequence, their early sexual experience contrasts sharply with the marked decline in their sexual interest after the disappointments with men that are their usual lot.

6

Three Suicidal Adolescents

Two of the suicidal patients were adolescents who had been considered juvenile delinquents. The third adolescent is the victim of the delinquency of a city institution, a hospital that dealt with him. Most discouraging about all three is that despite their youth there is nothing in their stories to give much hope that they can change the direction their lives are taking. All three stories, sad as they are, will not seem unusual to anyone familiar with the Harlem ghetto.

While in the "dungeon" of a police precinct, Eddie Marker, a medium-dark boy of eighteen, tried to hang himself. Earlier that day Eddie had been arrested on suspicion of robbery and as a result of his imprisonment had been twenty-four hours without the heroin he usually takes at the rate of seven or eight bags a day. Unable to endure the chills and abdominal pain of withdrawal, Eddie warned the guard that he would harm himself if he were not given something. Making a rope of his jacket and tying it to the ceiling ventilator, he hanged himself. When the guards found him and cut him down he was unconscious.

Eddie is on a forty-five-dollar-a-day drug habit. He has been a drug addict for the sixteen months since he was discharged from prison. He was sentenced on what he states was a false rape charge made by a girl who was jealous because he was not more interested in her. Arrested now for robbery with a gun he claims was only a toy, he has committed many burglaries to obtain money for heroin. Before he was sixteen Eddie had already been arrested for fighting and purse-snatching and had spent time in a detention home.

Eddie was the fourth of seven children. He describes his father as a strict man who would whip him with a strap if he did not do the right thing. He says he was not bothered by the whippings and that he fought with his father often. His father also encouraged him and his brothers to fight it out if they had a disagreement.

If his mother scolded him, Eddie would, and still does, cry. He wishes he were not on drugs for her sake since he feels she struggled to raise him. When he was not in jail, he lived at home until three months before his suicide attempt. Because his mother was afraid that his drug habit would have a damaging effect on the younger children, he went to live with his aunt. Eddie has a married brother of twenty-four who is on drugs but who never allowed Eddie to take them. Four months ago this brother was sentenced to three years' imprisonment for armed robbery. A year ago his twenty-two-year-old sister was sentenced to two years for homicide; she had killed their father, who she felt was trying to harm her baby. Although Eddie fights with a younger brother of seventeen, he feels protective toward him and tries to keep him from taking drugs.

When he was sixteen Eddie and a girlfriend had a child who is now living with her mother. His present girlfriend,

Eugenie, gave birth to his second child three months ago. Eddie says he would like to marry her but avoids her because of his habit.

He related the following recent dream:

> He found money in a trunk. He married Eugenie. She was unfaithful. He fought with the other guy. He was cut up and in the hospital. Eugenie came and awakened him.

His feelings toward Eugenie parallel those toward his mother. He sees drugs as separating him from both of them, yet at the same time he has made drugs a substitute for them. His mother has rejected him by asking him to move out to protect his brothers. He perceives this as a kind of infidelity on her part. He sees himself as losing out to his brothers in the struggle for her but dreams, significantly in terms of his suicide attempt, that his injuries will bring her back. In actuality, money, which for Eddie would have to be "found" or stolen, brings him not his mother or Eugenie but his substitute for them, drugs.

Eddie does not believe in death, and thinks his father is alive and that he will meet him again someday. For several years he and his younger brother have been Muslims. He says that now he is a "brother" and can do what he chooses, whereas the ordinary Muslims are only followers. He feels there is no God—a belief that makes him feel free.

In discussing his quick temper and his fighting, Eddie says he does not like to be pushed around. He gives the feeling of great potential for violence, although he seems to underestimate it. Eddie doubts that he will attempt suicide again, but he says he cannot be sure that he can break his habit. He has no plans for the future after he gets out of jail.

Eddie was returned to prison before a detailed exploration of the psychodynamics of his case could be completed.* Yet in one sense his behavior is his story—drugs, violence, robbery, illegitimate children—a story of life lived from day to day by a young man who has abandoned any hope of shaping his future.

When Eddie was asked about his getting into so much trouble he replied, "No more than most of the people I know." He told of a family next door with five children, all of whom were or had been in prison.

The ease with which ghetto life encourages moving in antisocial directions has been graphically described by Claude Brown, Malcolm X, and many others. While Eddie did not seem to be a great suicidal risk, his entire life appeared to be charted on a self-destructive course that was at least of equivalent danger to him.

Eddie uses his Muslim beliefs not simply to deny death but to deny the reality of life as he experiences it. He insists that his religion makes him free, yet freedom is literally and figuratively what he least has. Nor can he use the Muslim movement, as do others in this study, to try to control his drug habit or curb his criminal activities. Instead he contents himself with the self-deception that, as a "brother," he is superior to whites and blacks alike.

One hour after her boyfriend told her he was interested in another girl and would not see her any more, nineteen-year-old Vera Burroughs took twenty sleeping pills. Although she left no note and denies making any current threat of suicide, Vera had told her boyfriend a year be-

* His return to prison also made it impossible to administer psychological tests.

fore that she would kill herself if he ever left her. She claimed that her boyfriend's announcement was a complete shock to her, but she eventually admitted that he had been seeing her less frequently for the past few months.

Depressed and sullen in the hospital, Vera answered questions reluctantly and gave the impression of being angry with the world. During her first interview she expressed most emotion when saying that she never knew her father. She was born in North Carolina when her mother was only thirteen. Although she insisted that her parents were married, Vera's mother says this is not so and that she and Vera's father separated when her daughter was two or three. She then took Vera to New York to live with her own mother and three sisters. While Vera's mother worked, Vera was cared for by her grandmother.

Seven years ago Vera's mother married. Vera and her stepfather, Danny, quarreled a lot because, Vera explained, he was strict with her, never believed her, and whipped her with a strap. Vera feels her mother always sided with him and was less involved with her than she had been. Because she was unable to get along with Danny, Vera returned to her grandmother's apartment in New York. As soon as possible Vera dropped out of school and has worked irregularly as a domestic, quitting whenever she accumulated a little money. In general Vera gives the impression of having a great deal of difficulty in sustaining any effort.

An attractive woman of thirty-two, Vera's mother gives a different picture of her daughter, a picture that Vera eventually confirmed. All through school Vera had been in trouble for staying out nights with a group that indulged in petty crime and for being sexually involved in a "chain gang" in which she was passed from man to man. She had spent two months in a youth home. Vera's mother explained that both she and her husband worked nights and were not able to supervise Vera during the evening. Vera has been spanked only when she stayed out all night. It is clear, however, that her mother has little interest in Vera.

While Vera is reluctant to talk of the events that led to her going to the youth home, she is quite able to talk of the fights she has had. During a fight with another girl when she was seventeen, Vera picked up a knife but was talked out of using it by a friend. She then fought the girl without the knife and is quite proud of the fact that she won. She tells in some detail of beating up another girl only a year ago. The girl had started a fight when she saw Vera talking to her boyfriend. Vera feels she wins all the fights she has with other girls.

Both Vera and her mother agree that she was never in trouble before she was twelve, although Vera is more specific in dating her difficulties to the arrival of Danny. "No man not my father has the right to beat me." She feels that whatever she had of her mother was lost when her mother became involved with Danny.

Vera's first serious boyfriend was someone she saw for a year and a half in New Jersey. When she moved back to New York he made no effort to see her, nor she him. She tries to deny that she was hurt by his rejection.

Vera says that she has discontinued the sexual promiscuity of her adolescence. She feels she seldom has enjoyed sexual relations, even with her present boyfriend. She often dreams of a man who is after her with a knife and is able to sleep only when she puts a Bible under her head.* Although she believes in God, Vera is not actively involved with the church.

* Psychological testing suggested that although the patient might act quite unconventionally in matters related to sex or aggression, she manifested a tie to religion. For example, in one TAT story a boy has bad dreams of two men trying to cut him "so he went to church this particular Sunday and he wanted the minister to pray for him so that he wouldn't have any more bad dreams." On the tests the patient showed few assets. She scored at the borderline level of intelligence, with an IQ of 73. On the Rorschach test, her percepts were idiosyncratic and un-

Vera's use of denial to handle painful rejections is striking. She insists that she was not hurt by her first boyfriend's rejection of her, that she had not been aware of her current boyfriend's loss of interest, and that her mother and father were married, although she has been told that this was not the case.

Vera says she wants to marry, but feels this will occur in the remote future when she "grows up." Despite a sullen, seemingly independent façade, it is clear that she visualizes herself as an angry little girl.

Although Vera has managed to curb her asocial behavior, she appears to be paying a high price for doing so. The violence, petty crime, sexual promiscuity, and open defiance of her mother that characterized her rebellious adolescence have now subsided into a somewhat withdrawn, chronic sullenness. She resembles Eddie Marker in living from day to day with little involvement in shaping her own life. In their life stories, in their frustration and rage, and in their resignation and despair, both Eddie and Vera are earlier versions of the young adults between twenty and thirty already described in this study.

Although the last patient is also an adolescent, he is far from being a delinquent. He appears to have had bright prospects prior to the tragedy that changed his life.

---

conventional, reflecting unusual thought processes. Even in structured situations where cues for appropriate social action are obvious, the patient failed to perceive what other people usually see. However, she verbalized a strong desire for marriage and home and also indicated: *Sexual intercourse:* "This is a nature performance which God has given us to go and earn a family."

Luke Dellins, a dark-skinned high-school student of sixteen, slashed his wrists and stabbed himself near his heart. He made his attempt at night when the rest of the family was asleep and he lay in bed. In the morning his father discovered him.

Surly and evasive, Luke replied to questions with hostile or sarcastic remarks such as "Why do you want to know?" or "It's in the chart!" During his stay in the hospital several psychiatrists tried to treat him but without success. He remained sullen, evasive, and inaccessible. His particular bitterness toward doctors, understandable in the light of his story, contributed to his angry isolation.

Luke said he wished to die because of the pain in his leg, which he has endured since he fractured his right hip three years ago. The fracture was poorly set in a city hospital. A subsequent operation in the same institution made it worse. Eventually atrophy of the hip bone set in. A final attempt at repair left him with chronic pain and a permanent limp.

Having planned his suicide attempt for some months, Luke had waited for his junior year to end and evidently anticipated with some dread the freedom of the summer months. He had done well in school and had been very active in competitive sports before his injury. He had one sexual experience before his fracture, but says he gave everything up because now he cannot go anywhere or do anything. Since his injury he has withdrawn from his friends, both male and female.

Feeling that his leg is his only problem, Luke claims to be no longer interested in suicide because his pain has been eased by treatment in the hospital. Although he denies being equally disturbed by his limp, he dreams of himself on crutches in the rain, rushing to come indoors, but unable to move quickly. Luke goes from denying being upset by his limp to talking of his ardent black nationalism; his only hero is Jomo Kenyatta. Black nationalism and black power appear to help him to deny the impotence he feels in connection with being crippled.

Luke remained extremely angry in the hospital. Since he had not been a problem in school, nor used drugs, nor been involved in crime, he evidently had some control over his anger. His rage seems to have been aroused by any attempt by either black or white doctors on the ward to get close to him.

Luke gave little meaningful comment on his family, which consisted of his father, who is a longshoreman, his mother, a sister of fourteen, and a brother of nine. Because he wished to be discharged from the hospital his mother eventually signed him out. She missed appointments with me and with the ward doctors, but in talking to her on the telephone it was clear that she blamed herself for not getting Luke better medical care and would do whatever he asked by way of atonement. She confirmed that he had had no difficulty before his leg injury.

Although he refused to take psychological tests, his better-than-average intelligence was manifested in the verbal fencing with which he warded off contact. It is not possible now to assess Luke's functioning prior to his leg injury, nor is this relevant to our present purposes. While Luke's story might seem a kind of accidental tragedy, anyone working for a while in Harlem soon comes to learn that it is the kind of tragedy that happens so much more often in the ghetto than anywhere else.

Eddie's and Vera's delinquency has its source in the nexus of frustration and rage that lie at the core of many of the previously described patients, men and women whose lives suggest the possibilities available to the young. While all three adolescents are in a sense victims of ghetto life, their actions show the degree to which the injustices of an outer world, whether embodied in the family or in wider social institutions, have been absorbed into their own style of living—a style in which they do constant injustice to themselves and work outrage on their own lives. In the light of the earlier psychodynamic studies the events of these three lives take on an added meaning and depth.

At eighteen Eddie has fathered two children he cannot face and has virtually committed himself to the destruction of his body by drugs and of his life by the intermittent imprisonment he can expect for the crime necessary to support his habit. Vera, whose mother bore her at thirteen, herself entered a world of impersonal sexuality and petty crime when she was barely in puberty. Since Eddie and Vera have scarcely emerged from a childhood in which they felt rejected and denied, and have been overwhelmed by an adult world of violence and crime, it is not surprising that their hopes have been so soon exhausted or that they have passed from youth to age so quickly. As Luke feels his life is over at sixteen because of a now irreparable hip broken as much by the ghetto as by anything else, so do Eddie and Vera feel that their lives have been damaged beyond repair.

7

Conclusion

SINCE the approach to suicide of this study and that done in Scandinavia* is so much at variance with the sociological approach to suicide, some discussion of contemporary sociological thinking about suicide seems desirable. Most such work derives from the work of Emile Durkheim,† whose brilliance seems at times to be clouding rather than illuminating the vision of his followers.

Durkheim related suicide to social integration and social status. He concluded that the greater the social integration of the person through such institutions as marriage and the church, the less frequent the occurrence of suicide; the higher the person's status, the greater the danger of loss of status and the more likely subsequent suicide. Urban suicide rates should be higher than rural

* Herbert Hendin, *Suicide and Scandinavia* (New York: Grune & Stratton, 1964).

† Emile Durkheim, *Suicide* (Glencoe, Ill.: The Free Press, 1951).

rates because there is less social integration in the cities. Suicide rates should be lowest among the poorest social classes. While these observations are true for the European countries Durkheim described, experience in the United States has contradicted them. The rural suicide rate in the United States is now as high as the urban rate —indeed, in the last census year it was higher. Moreover, in the United States the highest suicide rate is found among the lowest social classes.

Because of discrepancies such as this between the actual and the postulated, sociologists have been attempting to accommodate and revise Durkheim's theories so as to cover all available data. These efforts, from Halbwachs* to Henry and Short,† seem to aim at finding propositions about suicide that will be true for all cultures at all times. As Gibbs states in his recent book of collected papers on suicide:

> . . . the ultimate goal is a theory that applies to each form or variation *within and among all* societies. To illustrate, a very unusual pattern is found in suicide rates by age in Japan. The rate increases to a very high level up to ages 20–24, then declines substantially, but only to rise sharply again among the elderly. Now this pattern calls for explanation, but the explanation should not be *ad hoc,* meaning limited to Japan. It should be derived from a theory about all kinds of differences in the suicide rate, not just in Japan but in other countries as well.‡

Most of these theories are based on efforts to relate data about suicide and other variables—namely, age, sex,

* Maurice Halbwachs, *The Causes of Suicide* (Paris: Alcan, 1930).

† Andrew Henry and James Short, *Suicide and Homicide* (Glencoe, Ill.: The Free Press, 1954).

‡ Jack P. Gibbs, ed., *Suicide* (New York: Harper & Row, 1968), pp. 25, 26.

marital and social status, alcoholism, and homicide—in a framework that will explain all of the data with a few central theories. Somehow the idea that suicide, homicide, or even age, sex, and social status can have different meaning and significance in different cultures never seems to enter such work.

In one of the most recent of the sociological reformulations of Durkheim, Gibbs and Martin relate the suicide rate to the stability of social relations and correlate more instability with more suicide.* By relating suicide to disruption in social relations, Gibbs and Martin hope they have a theory that can explain both variations in suicide rates and individual suicide.

By the time one reaches a formulation as general as "disruption in social relations," one has a formulation vague enough to cover many situations but so general as to be meaningless. Even so, the formulation is contradicted by the Negro experience, for if disruption in social relations were the central factor in suicide, the black population of all ages would have a suicide rate ten times that of the white population.

Studies that take statistical data based on status or social integration and formulate theories that cover all cultures and subcultures reflect a rigidity and a sterility that unfortunately characterize much of contemporary sociology. It is understandable why Durkheim viewed society in this way, for cultural anthropology was virtually nonexistent in his time. More disappointing has been the resistance of contemporary sociology to understanding the developments in cultural anthropology over the past forty years.

Much of the time society as viewed by sociologists seems to be a collection of age groups, sex ratios, and social statistics. Somehow the influence of each society's

* Jack P. Gibbs and Walter T. Martin, *Status Integration and Suicide: A Sociological Study* (Eugene: University of Oregon Press, 1964).

institutions in determining what kind of human being is shaped by the particular society is lost in the process. The search for theories that will explain Eskimo suicide in the same terms as United States suicide is a search for fool's gold—if you find it you have nothing of value.

The sociological work that has dealt most specifically with Negro suicide has been that of Warren Breed, who studied the problem of Negro suicide by interviewing the friends and relatives of forty-two black men who killed themselves in New Orleans.* He stressed the frequency of problems Negro suicides have with the police or other authorities, such as courts and welfare agencies. Breed feels that fears of the police and feelings of impotence in dealing with all the authorities were critical in these cases. These fears are based on the unjust, arbitrary, and often extralegal authority that the police maintain with regard to the black man, particularly in the South.

Breed borrows a seldom-used category of suicide described by Durkheim as "fatalistic." Durkheim says of fatalistic suicide:

> . . . there is a type of suicide the opposite of anomic suicide, just as egoistic and altruistic suicides are opposites. It is the suicide deriving from excessive regulation, that of persons with futures pitilessly blocked and passions violently choked by oppressive discipline. It is the suicide of very young husbands, of the married woman who is childless. . . . But it has so little contemporary importance and examples are so hard to find aside from the cases just mentioned that it seems useless to dwell upon it. However, it might be said to have historical interest. Do not the suicides of slaves . . . belong to this type, or all suicides, attributable to excessive physical or moral despotism? To bring out the ineluctable and inflexible nature of a rule against

* Warren Breed, "The Negro and Fatalistic Suicide," unpublished manuscript, Tulane University.

which there is no appeal, and in contrast with the expression "anomy" which has just been used, we might call it fatalistic suicide.*

Breed feels that Durkheim underestimates the frequency of this form of suicide. Some of Breed's cases were in trouble for nothing worse than traffic violations. Others were being sought in connection with more serious crimes. What he feels is central, however, is the black person's feeling of impotence in dealing with arbitrary authority.

Since his study of blacks who are already dead is based on interviews with their friends and relatives, it cannot deal with the adaptive factors that are likely to be of significance in such suicides. Difficulty with the police or other authorities was present in many of the subjects of this study, but psychoanalytic study of these cases leads to some rather different observations and conclusions.

Although the subjects in this study who swing over the narrow border between homicide and suicide have had frequent trouble with the police, their own feelings about their murderous impulses are more crucial than their fear of police punishment. For the older men whose adaptation had been characterized by submission and compliance, and whose lives had been previously free of difficulties with the police, the situation is still different. Their obedience and submissiveness served to mask rage and guilt that are significant even though not overtly expressed. Here the issue is less fear of the police than of the failure of a previously successful adaptive system. Their guilt and fear of punishment relate clearly to internal feelings of rage and guilt that had little to do with the police. Unfortunately, such patients seem to feel they deserve punishment far in excess of what they actually face.

From the conviction that such punishment is deserved

* Durkheim, *op. cit.*, p. 276.

to anticipating it by punishing one's self is not so great a step. Even the one patient in this study who cut his throat while the police were waiting to question him about a numbers charge had been harboring almost delusional fears of police punishment based on a real or imagined minor offense committed twelve years earlier. His fears were clearly based on internal guilt rather than external danger.

None of this is meant to minimize the objective and rational fear that the black man has of the police. Nor do the problems with violence that have been described in this study make Breed's interesting findings seem surprising. Yet the evidence is against using this fear of police as a causative explanation of black suicide. If it were, black suicide would be a much greater problem than it is. Moreover, the objective, rational fear can serve as a convenient focus on which to project one's own private terrors. Much as many American Jews who were not directly affected by World War II will make German soldiers the symbolic focus of their nightmares, the fear and rage of the black man may converge on the police, who become a symbol of his torment.

A previous psychiatric study of Negro suicide* was done by Prudhomme, who concluded that race is not a factor in Negro suicide because the subjects he studied did not attribute their suicide attempts to racial problems. Such a conclusion is based on too circumscribed a view of what it means to be black in our culture and of the effect of culture on character. Nor would one expect a suicidal patient to be aware of how his life history, character, and motivation for suicide are in fact inseparably linked to his belonging to any racial or cultural group.

The Swedish suicidal patients studied in my previous work did not attribute their suicide attempts to being

* Charles Prudhomme, "The Problem of Suicide in the American Negro," *The Psychoanalytic Review*, XXV (1938), 187–204, 372–391.

Swedish. Their being Swedish, however, often involved emotional constriction and a life-or-death need for successful performance, and was a central part of their particular reasons and motivations for suicide.* The American Negro's life history, character, and motivation for suicide are inseparably linked to the experience of being black in our culture.

In the lives of the young adult and adolescent patients in this study, it is perhaps most apparent that the murderous rage and self-hatred that mark their suicide attempts are an integral part of their racial experience and form part of the burden of being black in America. If the Negro has grown up hating his mother and father for rejecting him and later feels bitter at society's rejection, he seldom sees beyond his own anger to become conscious of the ways in which society has shaped and directed his mother's and father's treatment of him and each other. In fact the culture's overt rejection of the Negro all too often reinforces feelings of rage and worthlessness that are already present—feelings that the culture, operating through the family, has insidiously helped to produce.

The Negro usually needs to repress an awareness that he has so blanketed his entire race with his own self-hatred that he loathes all the characteristics of blackness. Over and over the subjects in this study try to deny racial motivations for their feelings or behavior, although such motives are apparent. Even the man who insisted on having an operation to make his lips thinner denied that he in any way connected the size of his lips with being black. In their most repetitive self-images the patients saw themselves as black bugs or black rats. While these images were often dreamed of as symbols linking sexuality, destructiveness, and blackness, it is no accident that the symbols that come to them originate in the most despised

* Hendin, *op. cit.*, p. 2.

and unwanted living things in the Harlem tenements—the rats and the roaches.

For most of the patients the capacity for the expansive feelings of love, tenderness, and friendship has been crushed at its source in childhood. The emotions that remain to them are the rage and self-hatred that fill the lives of the young patients in this study. Many of these subjects came to life only through acts or fantasies of violence. In merely talking of past fights or brutality they become far more animated than usual. They see living itself as an act of violence and regard death as the only way to control their rage. Perhaps this explains the long periods of emotional death that punctuate their violent acts or the variety of deaths-in-life that they use to keep their anger in check. For many young blacks life seems to be charted on a self-destructive course—whether the route be drugs, crime, homicide, or suicide. Even the young homicide victims often appear not to be accidental victims but to be leading lives that seem destined to end violently.

The relation of race to self-hatred and violence was also particularly apparent in the suicidal black homosexuals who preferred white partners. They too felt the need to deny prejudice against their own race and made unconvincing attempts to rationalize the choice of a white partner. For them the homosexual act included a symbolic incorporation of whiteness—a whiteness that signified freedom from anger—and could, if only temporarily, relieve them of the pervasive feeling of being loathsome "black bugs." For those patients in whom the aspect of degradation was the key to the homosexual act, a white partner served to intensify their own sense of being dirty or degraded. For all the black homosexuals in this study homosexuality was an escape from the destructive heterosexuality invariably associated with the brutality of their black fathers.

It would seem that the least racial concern was demonstrated by the older suicidal men, whose attitudes toward race and toward life could be summed up in the statement of one of them: "If you do what you are supposed to do, no one will bother you." Although they did avoid conscious conflict about racial problems, their entire character formation, with its obedient, submissive adaptation, is a product of the racial situation that has prevailed in the United States. They are merely the more pliant victims of racial oppression, who would be classified by younger or more militant blacks as Uncle Toms. They become suicidal only when an adaptation that has been distinctly Negro in our culture begins to fail them.

The suicidal black women whose conflict centered on their guilt over their inability to raise their children are clearly a product of the black family situation, which in turn mirrors the racial oppressiveness of the culture. Certainly the maternal rejection stems in part from the economic pressure on a mother raising her children without a man to support the family. Equally important, the mother who has herself been neglected as a child finds it hard to react differently to her own children, no matter how bitter she is toward her own mother for comparable treatment.

Suicide attempts are usually considered to be precipitated by disappointments in work and career success or by disappointments in relationships with the opposite sex. This is often true because both work and relations with the opposite sex can be used to try to compensate for feelings of worthlessness deriving from childhood. When work or another person serves such a function, the individual is vulnerable to failure or rejection. The Negro experience in both areas is worth considering for what it reveals about the relationship of culture, character, and suicide, and because it points up the need to view suicide in its cultural context.

The Negro experience is particularly devastating in its effects on attitudes toward work. The younger black patients have great difficulty in sustaining interest in any sort of work. Having long since given up whatever career hopes or aspirations they had fantasized as children, they could not envisage a future in which their situation would improve through work. As one patient put it, there is "no place in the world for a fellow like me . . . always be on the same level."

In my study of suicide in Sweden a "performance" type of suicide was found to be prominent. It was seen in men who try to repair a self-esteem damaged in early life through a compensatory overinvestment in success at work or a career. Failure in these endeavors opens up the original injury and leaves them extremely vulnerable. Such performance suicides, although almost prototypes in Sweden, are common in the white population of the United States as well.

The possibility of work or career success is too limited for the vast majority of blacks to allow adopting this as a compensatory adaptation. The families of the urban blacks who were the subjects of this study would generally be considered at the bottom of any socioeconomic class scale or as working-class at best. Upward social mobility, with the exception of the man who became a doctor, was virtually nonexistent. The racial caste system operative in the culture was so much more significant for the patients in this study than class differences as to make any discussion of these differences unwarranted.

While it is difficult for the younger men to become involved in the kind of work available to them, the older, more submissive men have all worked hard and persistently. For all but the doctor this has meant acceptance of limited aspirations. One of them feels a failure because after a lifetime of work he has not been able to accumulate any money. But even in his case one is dealing more with the failure of his obedient adaptation rather than with the thwarting of a driving ambition that characterizes performance suicides.

The younger patients in this study rejected the challenge implicit in the TAT picture of the boy in front of the violin. The boy in their stories invariably did not want to play the violin and refused to do so. All of the older, compliant patients who had worked composed stories in which the boy does play with varying amounts of pleasure. Parents played a role in both groups of stories: defied by the younger group, they are obeyed by the older.

The older men in this study who worked well had fathers who had responsible work histories of which their sons were proud. The girls who completed high school were the few girls who had fathers at home and working. These observations merely confirm what is already known about the importance of the opportunity to identify with a working father.

The attitude of most of the blacks toward education parallels their attitude toward work. As they are growing up they cannot see the relevance of education to their everyday lives or realistically view it as a way of improving their condition. Many of them eventually come to feel differently, but by that time they have usually not developed the capacity for sustained effort or are cut off from educational opportunities.

This raises an objection to the psychological testing of blacks done in this and other studies. Intelligence testing in particular is a measure of the black person's equipment and capacity in dealing with the tools and symbols of the white world. Insofar as much of Negro life is lived in this world, such testing has, as Dr. Carr points out (see Appendix II), some relevance.

Much of Negro life, however, is not lived in the white world but in the ghetto, which has often been described as a jungle—a world of violence, drugs, murder, prostitution, and so forth. It takes a good deal of ingenuity to survive in such a world. The lives of Malcolm X and Eldridge Cleaver are but well-known examples of such intelligence and shrewdness. Our intelligence tests do not measure the black subjects' ability to master the environment in which most blacks spend most of their lives. Moreover, such intelligence is a relevant but ignored measure of a particular black person's ability to cope with the unfamiliar, given sufficient time and motivation.

The damaged self-image that the black person brings into adult life is no more likely to be improved by his relations with the opposite sex than it is by his experience with work or education. The maternal frustration experienced by both sexes operates to make them mistrustful. The absence of a father deprives the girls as well as the boys of knowing an idealized male in an effective and protective role.

Over and over the adult women tend to complain that their men are irresponsible and ineffective. Although this is certainly their expectation, it is also confirmed by their actual experience. Nor could most of them respond to an effective male, since their anger toward men tends to make the stronger male a frightening figure.

For their part, the men consistently complain that their women are untrustworthy and controlling. This too is their expectation, but this expectation also is confirmed by the reality of their experience. While part of the women are untrustworthy and controlling. This too is related to male ineffectiveness, the males as well as the females feel confirmed in their worst expectations.

Among the suicidal patients who are reacting to abandonment by the opposite sex, the psychodynamic theme that repeats itself is that rejection stirs up the wounds of earlier maternal rejection. What protects the black patients from more such reactions is, often, that they appear to engage in their relationships expecting less of the opposite sex than is true of comparable white patients. Many of them attempt a kind of detached involvement which insulates them both from deep feeling and from injury.

These attitudes toward the opposite sex naturally affect

sexual behavior as well. By the time most of these patients have reached their mid-twenties and have been involved with and disappointed in the opposite sex, there is a marked decrease in their sexual desire. The few patients who remain active sexually are those who are most detached in their involvements.

The above attitudes form a marked contrast to the early induction into sexual experience that characterizes ghetto life. A great deal of this early sexual experience is adolescent rebellion against a frustrating family situation. For girls as well as boys, however, sex has an entirely different and often less enjoyable cast when set in the context of adult life. The illegitimate children that so many of the patients have forces motherhood on girls who are not yet prepared for womanhood. Their inability to function as mothers further damages their self-image as women and makes sexual enjoyment less possible. For many a black girl, becoming an adult means exposing herself to the experiences her mother endured—a life of serial pregnancies and inevitable abandonments. In adolescence, when there are no expectations of an enduring relationship and no past of sequential disappointments in men, sex can be a kind of enjoyable play.

One senses that for many black men sex serves a double purpose. The children they father serve as living proof of their potency and also as a mark of their anger. Their abandonment of women, often when they are in the most helpless of conditions, may be a way of striking back at their mothers who rejected them or at the succession of aunts, grandmothers, or cousins who raised them; of figuratively screwing womankind and lodging a protest against their own lives.

In neither sex, nor friendship, nor work, nor even drugs do most of the patients in this study find any pleasure in life. To some extent this is a reflection of the repressed anger and blunted emotional life that characterize the depressed patient, but it also appears to reflect in a more extreme form the way in which pleasure is interfered with or diminished in the lives of non-suicidal blacks.

It does not seem surprising that suicide becomes a problem at such a relatively early age for the black person. A sense of despair, a feeling that life will never be satisfying, confronts many blacks at a far younger age than it does most whites. For most discontented white people the young adult years contain the hope of a significant change for the better. The marked rise in white suicide after forty-five reflects, among other things, the decline in such hope that is bound to accompany age. The blacks who survive past the dangerous years between twenty and thirty-five have made some accommodation with life—a compromise that has usually had to include a scaling down of their aspirations.

While little in his life experience as an adult does much to diminish the black man's rage and self-hatred, the political and religious black nationalist movements aim quite consciously at utilizing black rage and elevating black self-esteem. Insofar as these movements helped the subjects in this study identify some of the institutional sources of their frustration, gave group sanction for rage, and attempted to channel this rage in the direction of corrective action, they seemed to be both psychologically and socially effective. Insofar as the patients attempted to use Muslim beliefs or black nationalism to create a feeling of superiority to blacks and whites alike, they were, not surprisingly, unsuccessful.

The last patient discussed in this study, Luke Dellin, tries, through the power of black nationalism, to deny the impotence he felt at being crippled. In a figurative sense the use of religious or political black nationalism to deny a feeling of being crippled was true of other subjects as well. The power of real or threatened violence often gave the subjects the illusion of potency, but the damaged self-image that underlay such compensatory efforts could readily be discerned as continuing to plague the patient.

Most recently an attempt has been made to shape psychology into a mold more consistent with the needs of black nationalism. Grier and Cobbs,* two black psychiatrists, state that black mothers reject and castrate their sons in order to prepare them better for the life they will encounter in a white world. The black son, in their view, grows up hating his mother because he does not understand that she is motivated by a concern for his welfare. The formula that Grier and Cobbs suggest for a black psychological adaptation is a shift of anger from black mothers to white society. This formula, if ignoring the inner turmoil of the individual, may at least serve some useful social purpose.

In fact, as this and previous studies make clear, the mother's rejection and castration of her child reflect the way in which the mother herself was treated as a child, her attitude toward the father of the child, and the way in which these and numerous other factors contribute to her view of herself as a woman. Like all other children, those black children who have experienced the least rejection are best prepared to deal with the world, black or white.

People who hate their mothers—black or white—usually have good reason for doing so. Mother love is, unfortunately, no more exempt than work, sex, or anything else in Negro life from the past and present racial situation in this country.

Culture influences character by a complex psychodynamic process in which culturally induced family patterns play a key role in perpetuating problems.† Some blacks, Grier and Cobbs among them, resent studies that emphasize this role of the black family. While such studies have been criticized as seeking to impose white

* William H. Grier and Price M. Cobbs, *Black Rage* (New York: Basic Books, 1968).

† Abram Kardiner and Lionel Ovesey's *The Mark of Oppression* (New York: Norton, 1951) provides the best analysis of the ways in which racial oppression disrupts the black family and helps to perpetuate the black person's problems.

morality on the black community, behind such criticism is the understandable fear that focusing on the black family will provide an excuse to avoid action to improve the black man's position in society, an improvement which would, of course, do much to stabilize the black family. To deny psychological facts, however, no matter how well-intentioned the political motive, results only in propaganda. Pride based on such denial of reality only breeds insecurity and implies a lack of faith that genuine pride is a possibility. Sacrificing psychology to polemic also does a disservice to the great tradition of black psychologists and sociologists who have diligently studied the race problem in America.

The rage and self-hatred that are an integral part of the black family situation are inseparable from the rage and self-hatred that are the outgrowth of racial discrimination in a society that stimulates the black person's desires but blocks their fulfillment. Racial oppression institutionalized family patterns that served to make the black man feel that he deserved to be treated as he was being treated. The black revolution is attempting to channel the black man's anger away from self-hatred and toward effective action to improve his lot. If so much of the black man's behavior, including the riots in which he burns his own community, still seems self-destructive, the cases in this study certainly demonstrate that, in the black's attempt to cope with frustration and rage, his feelings of impotence and self-hatred often cause his anger to turn against himself.

APPENDIX I
Figures and Graphs

This appendix contains the results of a detailed study of white and black suicide in New York going back to 1920. This study was made with the help of the New York City Bureau of Vital Statistics.

The graphs for suicide make clear the point made in Chapter 1 concerning the high black suicide rate in the twenty-to-thirty-five age group, while the graphs for homicide indicate that this is the same age period in which black homicide reaches its peak. The psychosocial significance of these statistical relationships is discussed in Chapter 2, "Suicide and Violence."

A table showing the methods used by black and white suicides in New York City is also included. The high incidence of jumping among whites and blacks stands out, with the figure for blacks strikingly high. Discussion of this phenomenon appears in Chapter 1.

Suicides—New York City
Rates per 100,000 Population, 1920–1960

		Ages 10–14					Ages 15–19					Ages 20–24				
		1920	1930	1940	1950	1960	1920	1930	1940	1950	1960	1920	1930	1940	1950	1960
Male	White	0.0	1.0	0.1	0.6	0.4	5.6	5.5	3.0	4.7	3.2	12.1	14.5	8.8	8.6	11.7
	Black	0.0	0.0	0.0	2.6	1.4	0.0	0.0	3.8	4.8	7.6	35.6	21.6	17.0	9.4	19.0
Female	White	0.4	1.3	0.1	0.0	0.1	2.2	3.8	2.5	3.3	1.5	7.4	9.4	5.8	5.0	3.4
	Black	0.0	0.0	1.6	0.0	0.0	0.0	5.0	5.2	2.4	5.4	9.0	13.7	7.7	2.4	3.6
Total	White	0.2	1.1	0.1	0.3	0.3	3.8	4.7	2.8	4.0	2.4	9.5	11.8	7.3	6.7	7.3
Total	Black	0.0	0.0	0.8	1.3	0.7	0.0	2.8	4.6	3.5	6.4	20.1	17.1	11.2	5.2	10.3

		Ages 25–34					Ages 35–44					Ages 45–54				
		1920	1930	1940	1950	1960	1920	1930	1940	1950	1960	1920	1930	1940	1950	1960
Male	White	14.0	23.4	15.9	9.0	12.3	26.3	41.8	27.1	14.0	12.6	31.9	68.4	43.4	23.2	21.0
	Black	15.1	24.7	11.0	12.5	22.3	25.4	33.7	12.1	7.7	18.6	26.0	23.0	14.4	15.5	14.1
Female	White	9.0	13.5	9.4	5.9	7.2	13.4	16.6	13.4	9.8	7.4	13.8	18.9	18.0	11.6	10.2
	Black	0.0	7.8	5.0	5.7	5.0	0.0	6.4	6.6	3.4	9.9	0.0	3.9	12.3	4.9	4.4
Total	White	11.5	18.4	12.5	7.4	9.7	20.1	29.7	20.2	11.8	9.8	23.2	44.5	31.1	17.3	15.2
Total	Black	7.1	16.0	7.4	8.6	12.5	12.8	20.2	9.2	5.4	13.2	13.7	13.9	13.5	10.0	8.7

Suicides—New York City (*continued*)
Rates per 100,000 Population, 1920–1960

		Ages 55–64					Ages 65–74				
		1920	1930	1940	1950	1960	1920	1930	1940	1950	1960
Male	White	43.8	84.9	53.0	35.6	26.8	66.4	87.5	60.4	46.4	34.4
	Black	0.0	26.7	5.5	18.3	22.6	0.0	0.0	7.7	3.4	18.1
Female	White	19.9	21.1	17.4	12.0	13.0	11.9	22.2	18.0	17.5	15.4
	Black	0.0	0.0	0.0	4.4	3.7	0.0	0.0	0.0	2.5	4.7
Total	White	31.9	52.6	35.4	23.9	19.5	36.4	53.0	37.6	28.7	24.2
Total	Black	0.0	12.8	2.5	10.8	12.2	0.0	0.0	3.1	2.9	10.5

		Over 75					Total all Ages				
		1920	1930	1940	1950	1960	1920	1930	1940	1950	1960
Male	White	107.3	84.6	70.3	51.9	50.2	16.5	29.7	22.6	15.7	14.7
	Black	0.0	75.0	0.0	14.0	11.9	16.6	19.3	8.4	8.4	12.1
Female	White	23.1	26.6	20.1	17.2	14.8	7.6	10.9	9.8	7.4	7.3
	Black	0.0	0.0	15.9	0.0	11.9	1.2	5.9	5.3	3.2	4.1
Total	White	58.2	51.2	41.4	31.9	29.9	12.1	20.3	16.2	11.4	10.8
Total	Black	0.0	25.3	10.9	4.8	11.9	8.5	12.3	6.8	5.6	7.8

MALE SUICIDES
New York City—1920
Age-Specific rate per 100,000 population

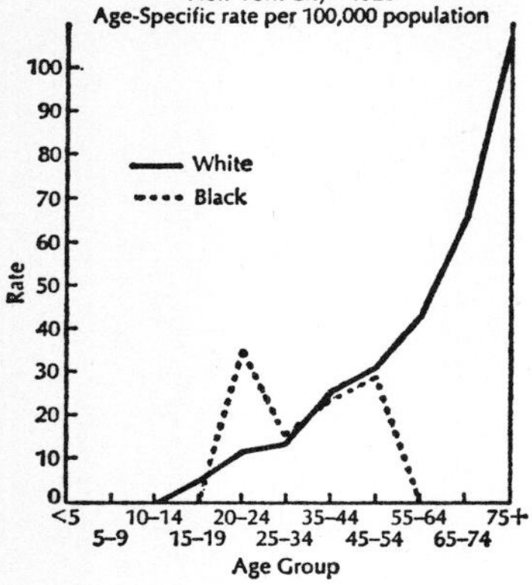

MALE SUICIDES
New York City—1930
Age-Specific rate per 100,000 population

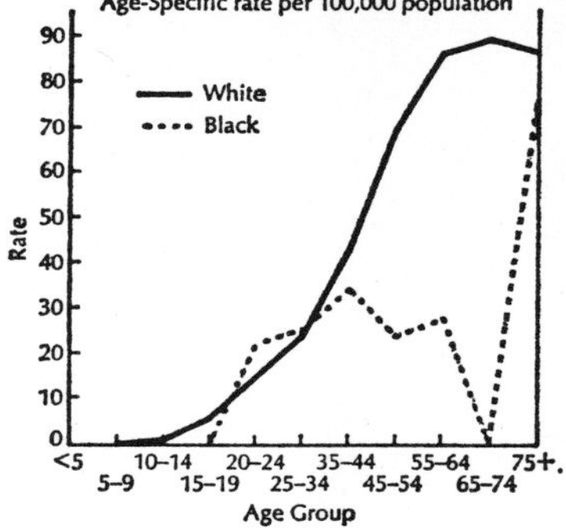

MALE SUICIDES
New York City—1940
Age-Specific rate per 100,000 population

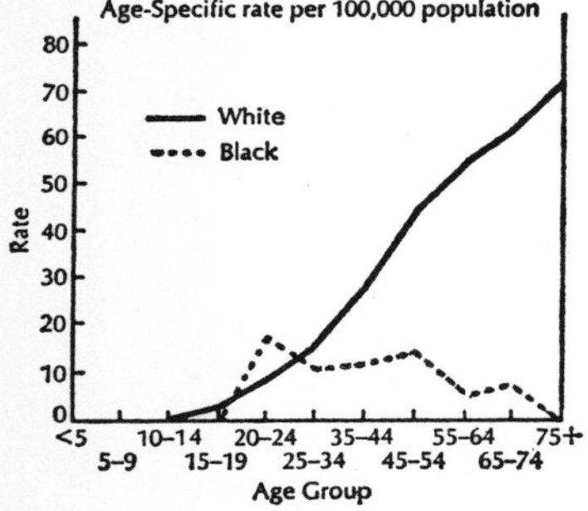

MALE SUICIDES
New York City—1950
Age-Specific rate per 100,000 population

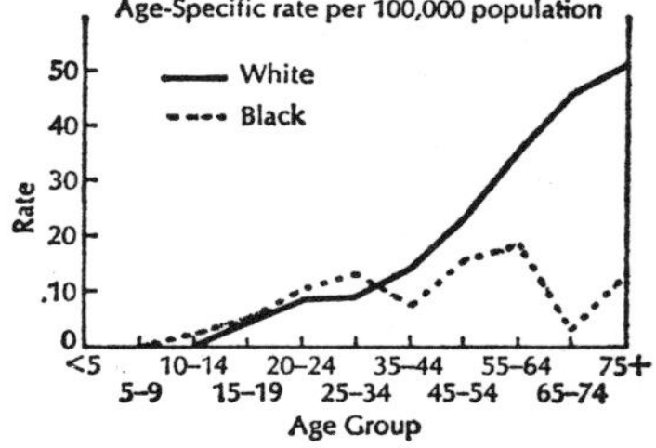

MALE SUICIDES
New York City—1960
Age-Specific rate per 100,000 population

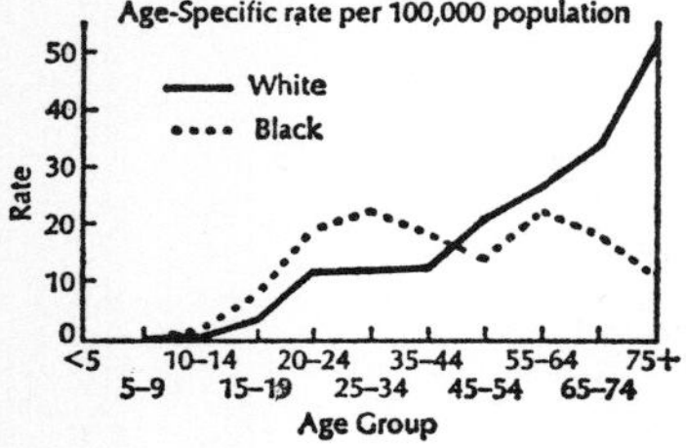

FEMALE SUICIDES
New York City—1960
Age-Specific rate per 100,000 population

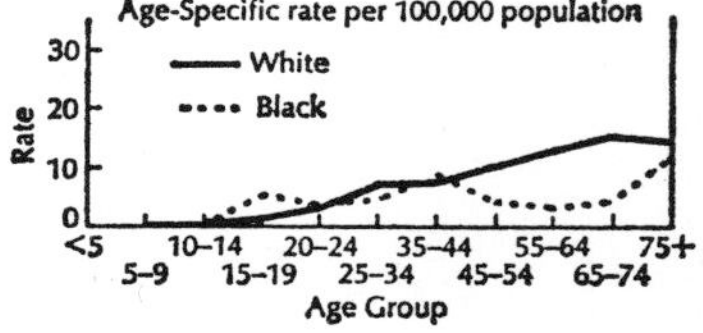

Homicides—New York City
Rates per 100,000 Population, 1920–1960

	Under 5					Ages 5–9					Ages 10–14				
	1920	1930	1940	1950	1960	1920	1930	1940	1950	1960	1920	1930	1940	1950	1960
Male White	2.2	3.3	2.6	3.2	2.5	0.8	1.3	1.2	0.8	2.6	1.2	1.2	0.7	0.6	1.3
Black	18.3	7.4	10.9	11.2	9.3	0.0	2.5	0.0	1.2	9.5	0.0	3.3	0.0	2.6	0.7
Female White	3.3	2.8	1.8	2.1	1.2	0.8	0.8	1.1	0.2	1.8	0.4	0.6	0.5	1.0	0.0
Black	17.6	11.9	4.0	6.0	3.3	0.0	0.0	0.0	0.0	5.4	0.0	3.1	1.6	1.2	2.9
Total White	2.7	3.1	2.2	2.7	1.9	0.8	1.1	1.1	0.5	2.2	0.8	0.9	0.5	0.8	0.7
Total Black	17.9	9.6	7.7	8.6	6.3	0.0	1.2	0.0	0.6	7.5	0.0	3.2	0.8	2.1	1.8

	Ages 15–19					Ages 20–24					Ages 25–34				
	1920	1930	1940	1950	1960	1920	1930	1940	1950	1960	1920	1930	1940	1950	1960
Male White	5.1	5.8	1.5	3.4	6.9	16.2	13.4	4.3	3.8	9.6	17.6	16.6	5.9	4.5	7.8
Black	73.4	43.6	46.9	46.2	41.5	59.3	90.0	54.4	68.9	48.3	55.3	81.6	75.4	54.3	66.1
Female White	1.3	1.4	0.6	0.5	2.1	2.1	3.7	1.8	1.6	2.2	2.1	2.6	1.1	0.9	2.0
Black	36.3	19.2	3.1	1.2	6.3	9.0	24.1	11.6	14.5	10.2	9.0	23.8	15.4	15.6	17.5
Total White	3.2	3.6	1.0	1.9	4.5	8.6	8.4	3.0	2.7	5.6	9.9	9.6	3.4	2.6	4.8
Total Black	52.1	29.8	23.1	21.7	22.4	30.8	52.5	27.5	36.2	26.4	30.8	51.6	40.1	32.1	38.4

Homicides—New York City (*continued*)
Rates per 100,000 Population, 1920–1960

	Ages 35–44					Ages 45–54					Ages 55–64				
	1920	1930	1940	1950	1960	1920	1930	1940	1950	1960	1920	1930	1940	1950	1960
Male White	10.6	12.9	5.3	3.5	5.8	8.5	11.5	5.3	2.5	3.5	9.0	7.1	3.7	3.9	3.6
Black	44.4	65.5	62.4	59.4	63.8	13.0	40.3	39.9	34.4	53.2	0.0	26.7	20.9	25.4	29.1
Female White	2.3	2.2	1.6	1.0	1.8	1.4	2.2	0.9	1.0	1.2	1.3	1.7	0.5	0.9	0.8
Black	6.4	14.8	12.5	12.7	17.2	0.0	3.9	7.5	4.9	7.4	0.0	3.8	2.4	4.4	3.7
Total White	6.6	7.8	3.5	2.2	3.4	5.1	7.0	3.2	1.7	2.3	5.1	4.4	2.1	2.4	2.1
Total Black	25.6	40.5	35.8	33.3	37.8	6.8	22.6	23.1	18.9	27.7	0.0	19.7	11.0	14.1	15.4

	Ages 65–74					Over 75					Total all Ages				
	1920	1930	1940	1950	1960	1920	1930	1940	1950	1960	1920	1930	1940	1950	1960
Male White	3.3	6.6	4.0	4.5	4.8	0.0	2.4	4.7	3.1	4.7	8.8	9.5	4.0	3.2	4.8
Black	0.0	22.4	15.4	22.9	26.0	0.0	0.0	0.0	28.3	25.8	38.8	53.8	43.4	38.3	37.4
Female White	1.4	1.2	1.0	0.4	1.0	3.8	1.8	2.2	2.6	1.9	1.8	2.1	1.2	1.0	1.4
Black	0.0	13.5	0.0	0.0	1.4	0.0	0.0	0.0	0.0	3.6	8.8	15.8	8.9	8.9	9.4
Total White	2.3	3.8	2.4	2.4	2.8	2.2	2.2	3.3	2.8	3.1	5.3	5.8	2.6	2.1	3.0
Total Black	0.0	16.8	6.2	9.6	12.1	0.0	0.0	0.0	9.6	11.9	23.0	34.0	24.4	22.1	22.2

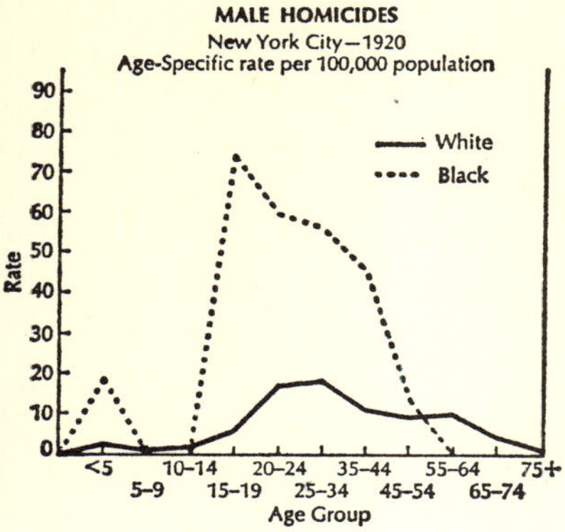
MALE HOMICIDES
New York City—1920
Age-Specific rate per 100,000 population
White
Black
Rate
0
10
20
30
40
50
60
70
80
90
<5
5–9
10–14
15–19
20–24
25–34
35–44
45–54
55–64
65–74
75+
Age Group

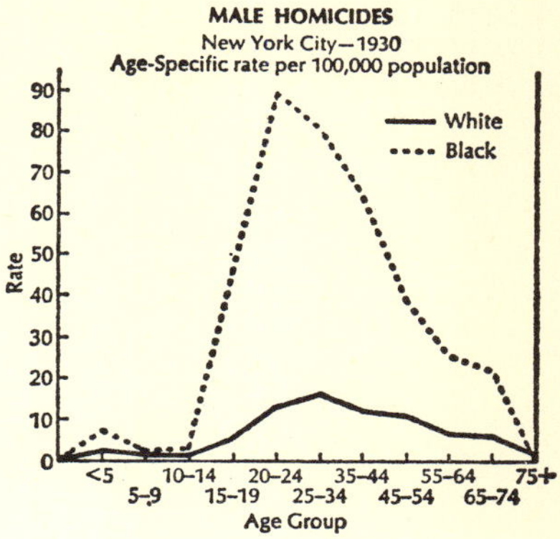
MALE HOMICIDES
New York City—1930
Age-Specific rate per 100,000 population
White
Black
Rate
0
10
20
30
40
50
60
70
80
90
<5
5–9
10–14
15–19
20–24
25–34
35–44
45–54
55–64
65–74
75+
Age Group

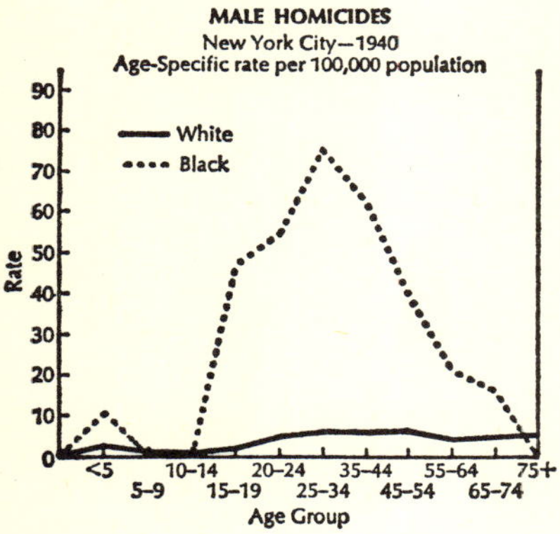
MALE HOMICIDES
New York City—1940
Age-Specific rate per 100,000 population
White
Black
Rate
0
10
20
30
40
50
60
70
80
90
<5
5–9
10–14
15–19
20–24
25–34
35–44
45–54
55–64
65–74
75+
Age Group

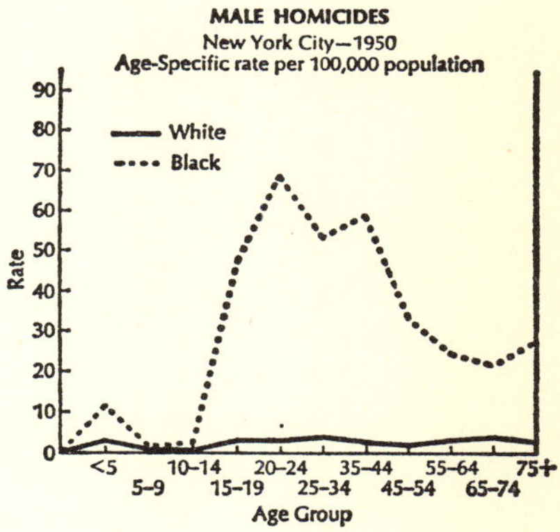
MALE HOMICIDES
New York City—1950
Age-Specific rate per 100,000 population
White
Black
Rate
0
10
20
30
40
50
60
70
80
90
<5
5–9
10–14
15–19
20–24
25–34
35–44
45–54
55–64
65–74
75+
Age Group

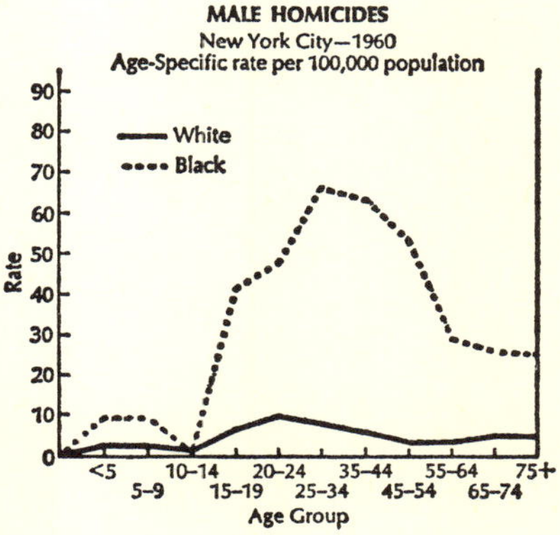
MALE HOMICIDES
New York City—1960
Age-Specific rate per 100,000 population
White
Black
Rate
0
10
20
30
40
50
60
70
80
90
<5
5–9
10–14
15–19
20–24
25–34
35–44
45–54
55–64
65–74
75+
Age Group

Black and White Suicide Methods—1960

	White Males	Percent of Total White Males	White Females	Percent of Total White Females	Black Males	Percent of Total Black Males	Black Females	Percent of Total Black Females
Jumping	150	30	88	34	35	56	15	63
Firearms	57	12	5	2	6	10	—	—
Hanging	130	26	33	13	6	10	3	13
Subway	16	3	5	2	1	—	2	—
Poison	67	14	81	31	5	8	3	13
Gas	24	6	6	2	1	—	1	—
Cutting	30	6	6	2	4	6	—	—
Drowning	5	—	12	5	3	5	—	—
Miscellaneous	15	3	23	9	1	—	—	—
Total	494		259		62		24	

APPENDIX II

Psychological Testing

ARTHUR C. CARR

Although comments on the psychological tests have been presented in the discussion of each case where relevant, it may be helpful to consider the test findings on the total group. The full battery included the following: Wechsler Adult Intelligence Scale (WAIS), Rorschach test, Thematic Apperception Test (TAT), Forer Sentence Completion Test (SCT), Draw-a-Person Test, and the Buss-Durkee Hostility Inventory. Testing was generally conducted concurrently with the interviews by Dr. Hendin. In many instances not all tests could be administered, because either the psychologist or the patient was unavailable at the time or because the patient did not have the ability to take a particular test. However, at least some of the tests were administered to twenty-two out of the twenty-five patients.

One of the major advantages of formal testing is the opportunity to compare the patient's performance with that of some larger reference group. Nevertheless, it should be made explicit that ideal norms are not available for purposes of evaluating suicidal blacks. What such norms should comprise would vary with the hypothesis being investigated. Is our comparison to be between suicidal and non-suicidal blacks, having the groups equated on all variables other than suicidal intent? Or is the most meaningful comparison between suicidal blacks and suicidal whites? Or should blacks be compared only with some other minority group? Regardless of one's wishes, norms on most tests are limited and any formal comparison which can readily be made can usually be challenged as also being of limited usefulness. To a large degree we are dependent on clinical inference as we approach much of our present test data.

With this limitation in mind, an attempt will nevertheless be made to summarize relevant characteristics of the group. Discussion of test results will be oriented primarily toward an illustration of the clinical impressions offered by Dr. Hendin and by an examination of some of the more widespread ideas regarding black people in our culture.

INTELLECTUAL FUNCTIONING

As indicated in Table 1, full-scale IQs range from 72 (borderline) to 115 (bright normal). One patient has a full-scale IQ at the bright-normal level (110–119), eight are within the average range (90–100), four are at the dull-normal level (80–89), and seven are at the borderline level (70–79). (On the WAIS, the IQ reflects a comparison of the individual with a standardization group presumably characteristic of the general population of the United States, chosen with proportionate representation with regard to such variables as age, sex, geographic region, urban-rural residence, race, occupation, and education.)

The revealed IQs of the patients obviously do not approximate a normal distribution—that is, if one were to draw a random sample of the population, it would tend to be higher than that obtained by our patient group. Undoubtedly some of the revealed deficit can be attributed to temporary influences such as fluctuating affective states, transient stress reactions, and rapport. It should be emphasized that a person's IQ does not represent his potential or past achievements but merely the level of present functioning. Nevertheless, on the basis of a theoretical framework consistent with the nature of the relationship between personality and intelligence, and using the individual as his own baseline, it can be inferred that the patients show liabilities that have time-spanning implications and that are not due to transient or situational factors. Inter-test and intra-test variability is marked and testifies to a general variability in functioning which would be manifested in and detrimental to the patient's adjustment. For example, an examination of the available range of information of most of the patients revealed few intellectual and cultural interests and a limited use of intellectualization. Great voids existed in relation to information commonly shared in our culture (for example, the source of rubber, the number of weeks in the year, or the date of Washington's birthday). The information subtest of the WAIS is, of course, far from being a culture-free test, in that performance on it, more than on any other subtest, is dependent upon formal educational opportunities and richness of life experiences. While some critics therefore challenge the fairness of such a test for disadvantaged groups, it should be stressed that the unfairness really exists in the life situation which gives rise to the disability rather than in the test, which is merely making it a matter of record.

Wechsler's definition of intelligence gives high priority to the ability to adjust, and his chosen subtests, including the information subtest, are consistent with this definition. It is a fact that a range of factual information, for example, is an asset in accommodating to our (or any) culture. Information regarding dates, places, people, distances, events—in short, how much one knows—represents a relative strength or weakness in the individual's mode of functioning and adaptation in relation both to other people and to the environment. So too with other abilities tapped by individual subtests on the WAIS, such as simple arithmetic calculations, verbal abstracting ability, psychomotor speed, and so forth. In view of the results obtained, it must be concluded that our patients are handicapped in their adaptational resources.

The limitations of the group were apparent in areas other than those subsumed in the concept of "intelligence." Projective test protocols (particularly the Rorschach test) were often extremely constricted, showing limited flexibility of response and few internal resources. For some patients (Harrison Eliot, James Redler, Edward Warner, and Barbara Weilen), the degree of impoverishment reflected in some tests, when taken independently, would raise a question of possible brain damage. The prevalence of violence in the background of some of these patients would make the possibility of brain damage more likely than usual.

In contrast to the impoverishment of many records, protocols of some patients presented a striking contrast between unrealized potential and present functioning. For example, while unable to solve relatively simple arithmetic problems, Leroi Nifson obtained an almost perfect score on the vocabulary subtest of the WAIS, correctly defining such words as "ominous," "tirade," and "encumber." On the SCT, he indicates: *People seem to think that I:* "am a rare avis"; *Most people:* "are brainwashed by the media, a political tool"; *Most marriages:* "are washed up on the shore of disgust"; *I used to daydream about:* "being a ruler of sorts and being remembered by History." What Leroi Nifson might have become, under other circumstances—preacher, politician, or even poet—leaves one aware of our shared loss which circumstances have imposed upon him and others in the group.

HOSTILITY

Because of the commonly assumed relationship between hostility and depression (as well as suicide), it appeared profitable to elicit from the patients some quantitative indication of hostility and its expression. For this purpose, the Buss-Durkee Hostility Inventory* was chosen, since it attempts to distinguish subclasses of hostility expression, such as assault (physical violence), indirect hostility (roundabout and undirected aggression), irritability (ease of provocation), negativism (oppositional behavior), resentment (jealousy and hatred of others), suspicion (distrust), and verbal hostility (anger expressed in style and content of speech). A total "hostility" score is thus obtained. In addition to 66 true-false items pertaining specifically to expressions of hostility, nine items elicit responses pertaining to guilt.

As indicated in Table 2, there is a wide range of scores in all categories. For example, in the assault category, scores ranged from 0 (Gloria Taylor) to the highest possible score of 10 (obtained by two females: Ina Tracy and Agnes Carreth). Any group average may thus be misleading. Formal comparison of these scores is also complicated by the unavailability of appropriate norms which would provide a fair comparison for these patients, as such an inventory is known to be susceptible to a response-bias associated with social-class status. Norms reported by Buss are for three college-student and two psychiatric-patient groups. Two additional groups of psychosomatic patients (neurodermatitis and glossodynia) have been accumulated by the present author from clinic patients who in terms of socioeconomic status would more closely approximate our patients. A selection of these groups is offered for inspection and comparison (Table 2). While none of these groups offers data for ideal comparison with our group of black patients, it can be seen that the total scores represented by the latter exceed those on any of the other groups. Furthermore, only in the black group do female "total" scores exceed male "total" scores and female "assault" scores approximate those of

* A. Buss, *The Psychology of Aggression* (New York: John Wiley & Sons, 1961).

the male. That reported "guilt" scores are also relatively high for the black patients follows logically.

Taken at face value, the evidence appears consistent with Dr. Hendin's clinical impressions regarding the presence of hostility in this group, and is strikingly relevant for the female as well as for the male. Somewhat disconcerting is the fact that even patients who scored relatively low on self-reported hostility expression (Peter Churney and Leroi Nifson, for example) give ample evidence from their history or from other test evidence that they nevertheless are motivated by strong aggressive impulses which present the threat of eruption. It appears that only Peter Churney's depression prevents what otherwise would be the breakthrough of violent impulses. By attempting to deny all feelings ("I don't have feeling; no sadness, no happiness. Never get angry. It's like I'm not in this world any more"), some kind of equilibrium is maintained, albeit an extremely precarious, circumscribed one. The most rabid racist could not constrict Peter Churney's freedom more.

In an effort to clarify the causes of the hostility of the patient group, SCT items pertaining to precipitating "causes of aggression" (for example, "I could lose my temper if . . ."; "I was most annoyed when . . .") were scored in terms of patients' responses. Response categories were taken from the Forer SCT check sheet and included: aggression (press), aggression (own), criticism, failure, health, sex, lie, rejection, unclear, denial, and omission. Of the group's responses, 33.3% were scored as aggression (press); 18.3% as "unclear" in meaning; 11.7% as aggression (own).

SCT items pertaining to "reactions to aggression" (for example, "When people made fun of him he . . ."; "After they knocked him down he . . .") were similarly examined and scored in terms of such categories as aggression, re-striving, depression, intellectualizing, avoidance, passivity, dependency, omission, or unclear. Highest response categories were depression ("cried," "felt badly") (33%) and aggression (22%).

SCT items pertaining to "causes of depression" were scored in terms of categories similar to those for "causes of aggression" (for example, "I was most depressed when . . ."; "I used to feel down in the dumps when . . ."). Highest response categories were "failure" (19%) and "inadequacy" (9%).

Although reservations must be placed on interpretation of these data, it would seem that, perhaps not unlike any other group, the patients view their own anger as instigated primarily by the press of other people's anger. Similarly, major responses to others' aggression are either depression or retaliatory aggression. Major causes of their own depression, on the other hand, were viewed as self-failure and inadequacy, seemingly an introjection of their own anger turned against the self.

ACHIEVEMENT MOTIVATION

Because of increasing interest in achievement motivation and particularly because of its relevance to the problems of the black person in our culture, it appeared desirable to obtain some measure of the patient's fantasy concerning achievement and the outcome resolution of such fantasy. For this purpose, each patient's story to TAT Card 1 (boy-violin scene) was scored in terms of the following variables: aspiration level (high or low), mode of resolution (active or passive), and type of resolution (success, failure, or none). In terms of these ratings, six patients (Ina Tracy, Andrew Vallen, Barbara Weilen, Gloria Taylor, Albert Mott, and James Redler) showed a high aspiration level while sixteen scored low on this variable. Of these six, however, only two (Gloria Taylor and James Redler) showed an active mode of resolution for this fantasy, and none of the six showed a resolution involving successful achievement. Of six patients who showed a successful achievement to their fantasy aspiration (Peter Churney, Eddie Marker, Leroi Nifson, Jean Wayne, Jeremiah Pitts, Edward Warner), all showed a low aspiration level initially. The picture that emerges is that, as a group, our patients showed no fantasied hope of success at a high aspiration level. Most frequently, aspiration level was low, mode of resolution was passive, and hope of success was poor.

THE ROLE OF THE FATHER

Studies of black people frequently stress the absence of the father in many black homes and the detrimental effect that this has, particularly on the young black male. In view of this frequently assumed influence, the stories to the so-called father-son card (7BM) of the TAT were inspected for male patients and scored in terms of whether the father-son theme was dealt with explicitly and whether the affect expressed toward the father-figure was positive (love, affiliation, trust) or negative (anger, negation, distrust). Seven out of ten of the males' stories to this card involved direct reference to father-son relationships. Only two, however (Jeremiah Pitts and James Redler), expressed positive affect.

Since with somewhat less frequency Card 6GF elicits father-daughter themes, the females' stories to this card were also considered. Stories were again scored in terms of whether they dealt with the father-child relationship and, if so, whether the affect expressed was positive or negative. Of eleven females, four dealt explicitly with father-daughter relationships. However, only one involved positive affect, and this was Alice Markens, whose father left the family when she was five and whose view of the father is obviously colored by fantasy and wish fulfillment.

While the above findings are admittedly inferential, it appears that these patients do not tend to view father-self relationships easily or in a warm, positive way.

SELF-IMAGE

In contrast to the direct evidence of feelings regarding self-image which is obtained in an interview and which is reported by Dr. Hendin, test results offer only inferential evidence regarding the self-image of our patients as blacks. In order to elicit themes dealing specifically with the patients' view of black-white relationships, TAT-like pictures were devised which showed blacks and whites in some interaction. Of 109 stories told to these pictures by a total of 21 patients, only 30 (27.5%) actually dealt with the race difference explicitly presented in the stimulus picture.

Since figure drawings are assumed in some way to reflect self-image, the drawings of the patients were rated in terms of the degree to which Negroid physical characteristics were projected onto drawings of either the same-sex or the opposite-sex figure. Of 15 patients from whom drawings were obtained, only one (Owen James) appeared to be attempting to represent Negroid features in both drawings. It is interesting that Owen James is reported as appearing white and as having been picked on by blacks for being white. Five others drew one of the two figures with characteristics (hair, lips, nose) that appeared to imply Negro identity. In no case did any patient attempt to convey the aspect of skin color.

There is little direct evidence in the test findings pertaining to the patients' attitudes about being black. (Atypically, Barbara Weilen reported on the SCT: *She felt proud that:* "she was black.") This fact is perhaps subject to varying interpretations.

On the one hand, it could be argued that it reflects the patients' denial of and reluctance to deal with such feelings, at least in the presence of a white psychologist, and that the lack of evidence directly suggesting pride in being black testifies to the loss which has been fostered onto our patient group. On the other hand, it may point out the irrelevance of skin color in relation to how the patients generally viewed their own difficulties and themselves, since only Owen James, who had a problem concerning racial identity, attempted to project such features in his drawings.

CONCLUSIONS

It appears that in general the test results are consistent with Dr. Hendin's major conclusions, suggesting that somewhat different motivations operate in black suicides than in other groups studied by him. These differences are related particularly to the role of hostility in the psychodynamics of the patients studied. The even broader implications of Dr. Hendin's findings stem from the assumption that patients serve as a barometer of the pressures existing on all people in a particular culture or subculture.

TABLE 1
Wechsler Adult Intelligence Scale Scores

Name	Sex	Age	Full IQ*	Verbal IQ*	Performance IQ	Information	Comprehension	Arithmetic	Similarities	Digit Span	Digit Symbol	Picture Completion	Block Design	Picture Arrangement	Object Assembly
Peter Churney	M	19	101	98	105	13	9	6	12	6	5	11	9	13	15
Harrison Eliot	M	33	72	71	77	7	7	5	5	2	4	11	5	7	5
Owen James	M	29	82	87	77	8	11	5	10	6	7	6	6	7	6
Ina Tracy	F	31	102	105	97	10	12	10	9	14	14	8	7	6	12
Agnes Carreth	F	22	95	91	102	9	7	9	8	9	13	9	10	11	9
Betty Scott	F	31	—	—	—	—	—	—	—	—	—	—	—	—	—
Alice Markens	F	23	83	76	95	5	6	5	6	7	8	8	9	11	11
Glenda Williams	F	29	78	82	74	9	8	7	8	4	7	7	6	6	4
Lorrie Peters	F	20	—	—	—	—	—	—	—	—	—	—	—	—	—
Leroi Nifson	M	20	103	110	93	14	18	7	9	10	8	11	7	9	10
Andrew Vallen	M	19	94	97	92	10	12	7	9	7	10	10	8	9	6
Benjamin Ellis	M	38	99	93	106	11	10	5	12	6	8	9	11	—	13
Albert Mott	M	40	84	86	84	7	12	7	6	6	4	7	6	7	10
Jeremiah Pitts	M	40	115	117	110	13	18	10	13	10	10	11	12	10	11
James Redler	M	68	96	99	92	11	6	12	6	9	5	4	7	6	6
Edward Warner	M	57	78	84	72	7	7	8	5	6	1	7	2	4	2
Louise Greene	F	26	—	—	—	—	—	—	—	—	—	—	—	—	—
Barbara Weilen	F	34	75	77	76	6	2	7	6	10	6	7	8	6	4
Willa Marsh	F	34	74	72	80	7	4	7	7	7	—	6	7	8	6
Marjorie Allen	F	20	89	83	99	8	8	5	8	6	8	7	10	10	15
Jean Wayne	F	17	92	99	83	7	10	12	10	6	7	6	7	9	7
Gloria Taylor	F	22	77	79	77	6	9	6	7	4	8	4	6	10	5
Eddie Marker	M	18	—	—	—	—	—	—	—	—	—	—	—	—	—
Vera Burroughs	F	19	73	78	69	5	5	5	7	7	6	7	6	2	5
Luke Dellins	M	16	—	—	—	—	—	—	—	—	—	—	—	—	—

* Prorated for vocabulary subtest.

TABLE 2

Buss-Durkee Hostility Inventory Scores

Name	1. Assault (10)	2. Individual Host. (9)	3. Irritability (11)	4. Negativism (5)	5. Resentment (8)	6. Suspicion (10)	7. Verbal Host. (13)	8. Guilt (9)	Total 1–7 (66)
Peter Churney	5	1	1	0	3	5	5	2	20
Harrison Eliot	4	3	7	2	6	8	11	7	41
Owen James	8	5	9	3	5	7	10	5	47
Ina Tracy	10	8	11	5	4	5	13	7	56
Agnes Carreth	10	7	10	4	5	5	13	5	54
Betty Scott	—	—	—	—	—	—	—	—	—
Alice Markens	7	5	9	2	4	5	9	6	41
Glenda Williams	4	4	6	5	4	5	4	9	32
Lorrie Peters	6	7	8	5	4	4	11	5	45
Leroi Nifson	3	3	2	0	2	4	6	1	20
Andrew Vallen	9	7	11	4	6	8	8	8	53
Benjamin Ellis	7	4	8	2	4	8	6	9	39
Albert Mott	6	0	1	1	0	3	4	2	15
Jeremiah Pitts	7	5	8	1	2	0	5	5	28
James Redler	2	1	3	2	4	4	7	9	23
Edward Warner	7	5	6	5	7	8	7	7	45
Louise Greene	2	0	1	1	1	2	2	5	9

TABLE 2 *(continued)*
Buss-Durkee Hostility Inventory Scores

Name	1. Assault (10)	2. Individual Host. (9)	3. Irritability (11)	4. Negativism (5)	5. Resentment (8)	6. Suspicion (10)	7. Verbal Host. (13)	8. Guilt (9)	Total 1–7 (66)
Barbara Weilen	9	7	8	4	1	2	11	9	42
Willa Marsh	6	5	8	5	3	5	8	8	40
Marjorie Allen	5	5	8	3	2	1	6	5	30
Jean Wayne	4	1	7	3	6	5	5	8	31
Gloria Taylor	0	4	8	1	5	7	5	8	30
Eddie Marker	—	—	—	—	—	—	—	—	—
Vera Burroughs	4	3	4	3	2	5	6	8	27
Luke Dellins	—	—	—	—	—	—	—	—	—
Average Scores									
Females (12)	5.6	4.7	7.3	3.4	3.4	4.3	7.8	6.9	36.5
Males (10)	5.8	3.4	5.6	2.0	3.9	5.5	6.9	5.5	33.1
Female College Students (88)	3.3	5.2	6.1	2.3	1.8	2.3	6.8	4.4	27.8
Male College Students (85)	5.1	4.5	5.9	2.2	2.3	3.4	7.6	5.3	31.0
Female Psychiatric Patients (114)	2.5	3.9	5.7	1.6	2.6	3.3	4.7	5.5	24.3
Male Psychiatric Patients (53)	3.3	3.6	5.0	1.6	2.9	3.3	5.3	5.6	25.0
Female Neurodermatitis Patients (15)	2.8	3.9	6.3	2.2	2.7	3.0	5.5	4.1	26.4
Male Neurodermatitis Patients (9)	4.3	4.1	5.3	2.0	2.6	2.7	6.2	3.7	27.2

Index

abandonment, 93, 105–106
abortion, 93, 117
achievement motivation, 161–162
aggression, 75, 90–91, 103 *n.*
alcoholism, 4, 15, 16, 17, 18, 19, 21, 30, 37, 39, 45, 46, 56, 57, 60, 72, 78, 81, 85, 88, 102, 107, 108, 112, 118
Allen, Marjorie, case of, 106–111, 115, 120
anger, 9, 10, 11, 15–18, 20, 22, 26, 27, 34–36, 36 *n.*, 38, 72, 76, 80, 84, 100, 100 *n.*, 108, 109, 110, 116, 120, 120 *n.*, 126, 128, 129, 130, 136, 138, 143–147, 160–161
animal phobia, 13, 14, 40–41
anomic suicide, 135, 136
Another Country, 70
anxiety, 60
atonement, 17, 28, 29, 36, 90, 91

Baldwin, James, 70, 71 *n.*
black attitudes, toward education, 142
black nationalism, 52, 129–130, 145, 146
Black Rage, 146 *n.*
black self-image, 162–163
black vs. white suicide patterns, 106–115
Breed, Warren, 135, 136
Brown, Claude, 7, 125
Burroughs, Vera, case of, 125–128, 130, 131
Buss, A., 159
Buss-Durkee Hostility Inventory, 11 *n.*, 20 *n.*, 24 *n.*, 27 *n.*, 40 *n.*, 52 *n.*, 67 *n.*, 76 *n.*, 100, 120 *n.*
Butts, Hugh, viii, ix

Carr, Arthur C., viii, 8, 142, 156
Carreth, Agnes, case of, 24–29, 32, 159
cases: Marjorie Allen, 106–111, 115, 120; Vera Burroughs, 125–128, 130, 131; Agnes Carreth, 24–29, 32, 159; Peter Churney, 9–15, 17, 20, 21, 52–53, 58, 59, 66–68, 160, 161; Luke Dellins, 128–131;

cases (*cont'd*)
Harrison Eliot, 15–17, 20, 21, 158; Benjamin Ellis, 60–68; Louise Greene, 94–96, 101, 120; Owen James, 18–21, 159, 163; Alice Markens, 33–39, 41, 44, 162; Eddie Marker, 122–125, 128, 131, 158; Willa Marsh, 101–106, 120; Albert Mott, 72–76, 80, 84, 161; Leroi Nifson, 11 *n.*, 49–54, 58, 59, 66–68, 158–161; Lorrie Peters, 41–44; Jeremiah Pitts, 76–81, 84, 85, 161, 162; James Redler, 81–85, 90, 158, 161, 162; Betty Scott, 29–32; Gloria Taylor, 116–120, 159, 161; Ina Tracy, 22–24, 28, 29, 32, 159, 161; Andrew Vallen, 54–59, 66, 67, 161; Edward Warner, 85–90, 158, 161; Jean Wayne, 111–115, 120, 161; Barbara Weilen, 97–101, 120, 158, 161, 162; Glenda Williams, 39–41, 44
castration, symbolic, 58–59, 78, 107 *n.*, 146
Causes of Suicide, 133 *n.*
childhood experiences, 15, 16, 19, 21–23, 28, 31, 32, 34–35, 38, 42–44, 74, 78, 80, 86, 94, 100, 103, 106, 108, 117–118, 123, 131, 139
children, 15, 18, 20, 21, 26, 29, 33, 36, 64, 93–98, 100–101
Churney, Peter, case of, 9–15, 17, 20, 21, 52–53, 58, 59, 66, 67, 68, 160, 161
Clark, Kenneth, viii
Cleaver, Eldridge, 142
Cobbs, Price M., 146
Cotton, John, viii
crime, 4, 10, 16, 46, 123, 125, 128, 131, 139
Cubbison, Patricia, viii
cultural maladjustment, 4
cutting, as suicide method, 49, 54, 66, 81, 85, 129

Davis, Elizabeth, viii
Dellins, Luke, case of, 128–131
delusions, 88–89, 90, 101
Denmark, suicide-homicide in, 46
dependency, 20, 24, 38, 42, 43, 44, 49–50, 66 *n.*, 107 *n.*
depression, 15
Diner, Martin, viii
Dollard, John, viii
Draw-a-Person Test, 156, 162
dreams, 13–14, 16–17, 23, 26, 27, 31–32, 34–37, 42, 43, 57–58, 64–66, 74, 83, 109, 110, 113, 114, 117, 119, 120, 124, 127, 129
drowning, as suicide method, 6–8
drug use, 10, 13, 23, 46, 97–100, 122–125, 131, 139
Durkheim, Emile: on fatalistic suicide, 135–136; theory of suicide, 132–134

Easser, B. Ruth, viii
education, 10, 12 *n.*, 19, 23, 25, 31, 39, 50–51, 54, 57, 63, 74, 78, 82, 86, 94, 109, 112–114, 118, 126, 129
Eliot, Harrison, case of, 15–17, 20, 21, 155
Ellis, Benjamin, case of, 60–68
emotional constriction, 26, 29, 32, 80, 84, 90, 95, 116, 120, 138, 144

family patterns, 146–147
fatalistic type of suicide, 135–136
father, 10, 14, 16, 19, 22, 25, 29, 31, 32, 34–35, 38, 42, 44–45, 50, 52–53, 56–57, 59, 66, 69, 70, 74, 77, 83, 84, 86, 90, 93, 99–100, 102, 104, 106–108, 111–115, 121, 123, 124, 126, 128, 130
father surrogate, 108–109, 126
Ferdinand, R. A., viii

figure drawings, and Negroid features, 162
Finland, suicide-homicide in, 46
Forer Sentence Completion Test, 12 *n.*, 15 *n.*, 20 *n.*, 24 *n.*, 36 *n.*, 56 *n.*, 76 *n.*, 82 *n.*, 84 *n.*, 96 *n.*, 101 *n.*, 103 *n.*, 112 *n.*, 119 *n.*; discussion of, 156, 158, 160
foster parents, 116–118
Frazier, E. Franklin, viii
Freud, S., 46, 48; on suicide, 45
frustration, 17, 58, 60, 72, 80, 101, 130

gas, as suicide method, 18, 19, 30
ghetto life, 7, 14–16, 139, 142, 144
Gibbs, Jack P., 133, 134
Giovanni's Room, 71 *n.*
Greenbaum, S. David, viii
Greene, Louise, case of, 94–96, 101, 120
Grier, William H., 146
guilt feelings, 23, 34, 40 *n.*, 93, 94, 96, 101, 105, 140
guilt test scores, 159–160

Halbwachs, Maurice, 133
hallucinations, 34, 39–41, 45
hanging, as suicide method, 30, 37, 122–123
Harlem, *see* ghetto
Hendin, Herbert, 4 *n.*, 132 *n.*, 138 *n.*, 157, 160, 162, 163
Henry, Andrew, 133; on suicide, 46–47
Herman, Morris, viii
heterosexual potency, 55, 62, 63, 69, 70, 71 *n.*
heterosexuality, as violence, 51, 53, 70–71, 139
homicidal fantasies, 11, 18, 24
homicide rate, black vs. white, 3, 5–6; in New York City, 5–6
homicide, and suicide, 3, 5–6, 46, 47–48, 139; in European countries, 46
homosexuality, 12–13, 15, 51, 55, 57, 59–68, 139; *see also* suicidal male homosexuals
hostility, 11 *n.*, 78 *n.*, 112 *n.*, 163
hostility index, 159–161
Hostility Inventory, *see* Buss-Durkee Hostility Inventory

imaginary voices, 33, 34, 38, 39, 40–41, 101; *see also* delusions, hallucinations
intellectual functioning, and tests, 157–159
intelligence quotients, 12 *n.*, 16 *n.*, 20 *n.*, 52 *n.*, 78 *n.*, 84 *n.*, 89 *n.*, 103 *n.*, 112 *n.*, 119 *n.*, 127 *n.*, 130; distribution and range, 157–158
Italy, suicide-homicide in, 46

James, Owen, case of, 18–21, 162, 163
Job Corps, 54, 57
jumping: defined, 6 *n.*; frequency in black suicides in Harlem, 6–7; as suicide method, 28, 29–30, 41, 70, 72, 101, 102

Kardiner, Abram, vii, 146 *n.*
Kenyatta, Jomo, 129
Klein, Milton, viii
Klineberg, Otto, vii

literacy, 12, 18, 19, 20 *n.*, 21, 103 *n.*

MacDonald, David, viii
Malcolm X, 125, 142
male sexuality, as violence, 52–53, 69
Manchild in the Promised Land, 7
marital relations, 15–20, 24, 26, 30, 32–34, 39–40, 60, 63–64, 66, 78, 81–82, 85–86, 90, 95, 97–98
Mark of Oppression, 146 *n.*
Markens, Alice, case of, 33–39, 41, 44, 162

Marker, Eddie, case of, 122–125, 128, 131, 158
Marsh, Willa, case of, 101–106, 120
Martin, Walter P., 134
maternal dependence, 49–50, 53, 80
maternal frustration, 75, 100, 143
maternal rejection, 20, 22, 26, 30, 53, 58, 93, 96, 110, 126–127, 138, 140, 143, 146
Moore, Austin, viii
moral form of suicide, 4, 91
mother, 11, 13–14, 15 *n.*, 16–20, 22, 24, 25, 27–29, 31–32, 34, 35, 37, 38, 42–45, 50, 53–55, 58–62, 69–70, 74–76, 78–80, 83, 86–90, 94, 97, 101, 103, 104, 106, 107, 109, 111, 113, 114, 118, 121, 123, 124, 126, 128, 130, 144
mother surrogate, 19, 25, 32, 39, 41, 42, 56, 59, 60–61, 78, 86, 90, 94, 103, 144
motherhood, 93, 96
Mott, Albert, case of, 72–76, 80, 84, 161
Myrdal, Gunnar, viii

"National Character," 4 *n.*
"Negro and Fatalistic Suicide," 135 *n.*
Negro vs. white suicide and homicide rates, 3, 5–6
Negro women, and suicide, 140; *see also* suicidal women
Negroes, older, and suicide, 139–140; and psychological tests, 142–143
Nelson, Freda, viii
Nelson, John, ix
New York City Bureau of Vital Statistics, 5
Nifson, Leroi, case of, 11 *n.*, 49–54, 58, 59, 66, 67, 68, 158–161
norms of psychological tests, 156–157
Norway: suicide in, 4, 6–7; suicide-homicide in, 46

Oedipal problems, in women's suicidal attempts, 112 *n.*, 115
Ovesey, 146 *n.*

paranoia, and suicide, 31
performance-failure type of suicide, 4, 91, 138, 141
Peters, Lorrie, case of, 41–44
Pettigrew, Thomas, viii
Pitts, Jeremiah, case of, 76–81, 84, 85, 161, 162
poison, as suicide method, 9, 24, 33, 39–41, 49, 60, 63, 76, 97, 103, 106, 111, 116, 125
police, fear of, and suicide, 136–137
pregnancy, 20, 23, 26, 33, 39, 93, 103–107, 144
"Problem of Suicide in the American Negro," 137 *n.*
prostitution, 98
Prudhomme, Charles, 137
psychodynamics: of suicidal homosexuals, 68–69; of suicide, 7, 45–48, 131, 143, 146–147, 163
psychological tests: achievement motivation, 161–162; anger, 160–161; and black self-image, 162–163; figure drawings and Negroid features, 162; guilt scores, 159–160; hostility index, 159–161; intellectual functioning, 157–159; intelligence quotients, distribution and range, 157–158; norms, 156–157; objections to, for Negroes, 142–143; racial identity, 162–163; tests used, 156; *see also* Buss-Durkee Hostility Inventory, Draw-a-Person Test, Forer Sentence Completion Test, intelligence quotients, Rorschach Test, Thematic Ap-

perception Test, Wechsler Adult Intelligence Scale
Psychology of Aggression, 159 *n.*
psychotic episode, 101, 105

racial identity, 14, 19, 21, 32, 40–41, 43, 44, 51, 54, 55, 58–59, 64, 65, 68–71, 74–75, 123, 137–140, 162–163
racial institutions, 7, 44–45, 47–48
rape, 123
Redler, James, case of, 81–85, 90, 158, 161, 162
rejection, 32, 67, 127, 128, 138; *see also* maternal rejection
religion, 26, 28, 37, 43, 45, 50, 53, 54, 56, 58, 59, 63, 103 *n.*, 107, 109, 117–118, 124, 125, 127, 127 *n.*, 145
restraint, external, and suicide, 47
Rorschach Test, 11 *n.*, 15 *n.*, 20 *n.*, 36 *n.*, 40 *n.*, 66 *n.*, 76 *n.*, 82 *n.*, 84 *n.*, 89 *n.*, 112 *n.*, 119 *n.*, 127 *n.*, 156, 158

Scandinavia, suicide in, 4
Scott, Betty, case of, 29–32
self-hatred, 106, 138, 139, 145, 147
self-image, 23, 138, 144, 145, 162–163
self-punishment, 89, 136–137; *see also* atonement
Sentence Completion Test, *see* Forer Sentence Completion Test
sexual experience, 12–13, 17, 19, 25–26, 35, 42, 72–73, 75, 77, 79, 82, 82 *n.*, 84, 87, 94, 95, 102–104, 108, 110, 112, 116–117, 121, 123–124, 126–131, 140, 143–144
Short, James, 133; on suicide, 46–47
siblings, relations with, 11, 13, 16, 27–29, 31, 35, 37, 42, 108, 123
social relations, 134
social status, 132–133
sociology of suicide, 46–48, 132–137
Status Integration and Suicide: A Sociological Study, 134 *n.*
submissiveness, 72, 75, 90–91, 140
subway, as suicide method, 72
suicidal male homosexuals: alcoholism, 56, 57, 60; anxiety, 60; black nationalism, 52; castration, symbolic, 58–59; children, 64; dependency, 49–50, 66 *n.*; dreams, 57–58, 64, 65, 66; education, 50–51, 54, 57, 63; father, relations with, 50, 52–53, 56–57, 59, 66, 69, 70; frustration, 58, 60; heterosexual potency, 55, 62, 63, 69, 70, 71 *n.*; heterosexuality, as violence, 51, 53, 70–71; homosexual experience, 51, 55, 57, 59–68; male sexuality, as violence, 52–53, 59; marital relations, 60, 63–64, 66; maternal dependency, 49–50, 53; maternal rejection, 53, 58; mother, relation to, 50, 53–55, 58–62, 69–70; mother surrogate, 56, 59–61; psychodynamics of black vs. white homosexuals, 68–69; racial identity, 51, 54, 55, 58–59, 64, 65, 68–71; rejection, 67; religion, 50, 53, 54, 56, 59, 63; suicide rates, black vs. white homosexuals, 68; violence, 56, 58, 69; work experience, 50–51, 54, 58, 63; *see also* Peter Churney, case of
suicidal men: aggression, 75, 90–91; alcoholism, 15–19, 21, 72, 78, 81, 85, 87, 88; anger, 9–11, 15–18, 20, 22, 72, 76, 80, 84, 126, 128–130; animal phobia, 13, 14; atonement, 17, 90, 91; black nationalism, 129–130; childhood experi-

suicidal men (*cont'd*)
ences, 15, 16, 19, 21, 74, 78, 80, 86, 123, 131; children, relation to, 15, 18, 20, 21; crime, 10, 16, 123, 125, 128, 131; delusions, 88–89, 90; depression, 15; dreams, 13–14, 16–17, 74, 83, 127, 129; drug addiction, 10, 13, 122–125, 131; education, 10, 12 *n.*, 19, 74, 78, 82, 86, 126, 129; emotional constriction, 80, 84, 90; father, relations with, 10, 14, 16, 19, 74, 77, 83, 84, 90, 123, 124, 126, 128, 130; father surrogate, 126; frustration, 17, 72, 76, 80, 130; homicidal fantasies, 11, 18; homosexual tendency, 12–13; hostility, 11 *n.*, 15 *n.*, 78 *n.*; literacy, 12, 18, 19, 20 *n.*, 21; marital relations, 15–20, 78, 81–82, 85–86, 90; maternal dependence, 80; maternal frustration, 75; maternal rejection, 20, 126–127; moral form of suicide, 91; mother, relations with, 11, 13–14, 15 *n.*, 16–20, 74–76, 78–80, 83, 86–90, 123, 124, 126, 128, 130; mother surrogate, 19, 78, 86, 90, 126; pregnancy, 20; racial identity, 14, 19, 21, 74–75, 123; rape, 123; rejection, 127, 128; religion, 124, 125, 127, 127 *n.*; self-punishment, 89; sexual experience, 12–13, 17, 19, 72–73, 75, 77, 79, 82, 82 *n.*, 84, 87, 123–124, 126–131; siblings, relations with, 11, 13, 16, 123; submissiveness, 72, 75, 90–91; violence, 9–17, 20, 20 *n.*, 21, 91–92, 123, 124, 125, 127, 128; work experience, 15–21, 72–74, 81, 85, 87, 126

suicidal women: abandonment, 93, 105–106; abortion, 94, 117; aggression, 103 *n.*; alcoholism, 30, 37, 39, 102, 107, 108, 112, 118; anger, 26–27, 34–36, 36 *n.*, 38, 100, 100 *n.*, 101, 107 *n.*, 108, 109, 110, 116, 120, 120 *n.*, 143; animal phobia, 40–41; atonement, 28–29, 36; black vs. white suicide patterns, 106, 115; castration, symbolic, 107 *n.*; childhood experiences, 22–23, 28, 31, 32, 34–35, 38, 42–44, 94, 100, 103, 106, 108, 117–118; children, relations with, 26, 29, 33, 36, 93–98, 100–101; delusions, 101; dependency, 20, 24, 38, 42, 43, 44, 107 *n.*; dreams, 23, 26, 27, 31–32, 34–37, 42, 43, 109, 110, 113, 114, 117, 119, 120; drug addiction, 23, 97–100; education, 23, 25, 31, 39, 94, 109, 112–114, 118; emotional constriction, 26, 29, 32, 95, 116, 120; father, relations with, 22, 25, 29, 31, 32, 34–35, 38, 42, 93, 99–100, 102, 104, 106–108, 111–115, 121; father surrogate, 108–109; foster parents, 116–118; frustration, 101; guilt feelings, 23, 34, 40 *n.*, 93, 94, 96, 101, 105; hallucinations, 34, 39–40, 41, 45; homicidal fantasies, 24; hostility, 112 *n.*; imaginary voices, 33, 34, 38–41, 101; literacy, 103 *n.*; marital relations, 24, 26, 30, 32–34, 39–40, 95, 97–98; maternal frustration, 100; maternal rejection, 22, 26, 30, 93, 96, 110; mother, relations with, 22, 24, 25, 27–29, 31–32, 34, 35, 37, 38, 42–43, 94, 97, 99, 101, 103, 104, 106, 107, 109, 111, 113, 114, 118, 121; mother surrogate, 25, 32, 39, 41, 42, 94, 103; motherhood, 93, 96; Oedipal problems,

112 *n.*, 115; paranoia, 31; pregnancy, 23, 26, 33, 39, 93, 103–107, 144; prostitution, 98; psychotic episode, 101, 105; racial identity, 32, 40–41, 43, 44; rejection, 32; religion, 26, 28, 37, 43, 103 *n.*, 107, 109, 117–118; self-hatred, 106; self-image, 23, 144; sexual experience, 23, 25–26, 35, 42, 94, 95, 102–104, 108, 110, 112, 116–117, 121; siblings, relation to, 27–29, 31, 35, 37, 42, 108; violence, 24–25, 27–31, 33, 35, 36, 38, 40, 41, 43–44, 103, 112 *n.*; visions, 35; work experience, 26, 30, 31, 33, 35, 39, 94, 98, 99, 102, 105, 107, 109, 112–114, 118, 120

Suicide (Durkheim), 132 *n.*

Suicide (Gibbs), 133 *n.*

suicide: alcoholism, 4, 45, 46; anger, 136, 138, 139, 144–147, 160–161; anomic, 135, 136; black attitudes toward education, 142; black nationalism, 145, 146; castration, symbolic, 78, 146; childhood experience, 139; crime, 4, 46, 139; cultural maladjustment, 4; drug use, 46, 139; Durkheim's theory of, 132–134; emotional constriction, 138, 144; family patterns, 146–147; father, relations with, 44–45; fatalistic type, 135–136; Freud on, 45; ghetto life, 139, 142, 144; guilt feelings, 140, 159–160; hallucination, 45; heterosexuality, as violence, 139; homicide, 3, 5–6, 46–48, 139; homosexuality, 139; hostility, 159–161, 163; maternal frustration, 143; maternal rejection, 138, 140, 143, 146; moral form, 4, 91; mother, relation to, 44–45, 144; mother surrogate, 144; among Negro women, 140; in Norway, 6–7; among older Negroes, 139–140; performance-failure type, 4, 91, 138, 141; police, fear of, 136–137; psychodynamics of, 7, 45–48, 131, 143, 146–147, 163; racial identity, 44, 137–140, 162–163; racial institutions, 7, 44–45, 47–48; rejection, 138; religion, 45, 145; restraint, external, 47; sample population studied, 7–8; in Scandinavia, 4; self-hatred, 138, 139, 145, 147; self-image, 138, 139, 145, 162–163; self-punishment, 136–137; sexual experience, 140, 143–144; social relations, 134; social status, 132–133; sociology of, 46–48, 132–147; submissiveness, 140; in Sweden, 137–138, 141; techniques for study of, 4; upward social mobility, 141; violence, 45, 139; work experience, 44, 140–142

Suicide and Homicide, 133 *n.*

Suicide and Scandinavia, 4 *n.*, 132 *n.*

suicide, methods of; black vs. white (table), 155; cutting, 49, 54, 66, 81, 85, 129; drowning, 6–8; gas, 18, 19, 30; hanging, 30, 37, 122–123; jumping, 6–7, 28–30, 41, 70, 72, 101, 102; poison, 9, 24, 33, 39, 40, 41, 49, 60, 63, 76, 97, 103, 106, 111, 116, 125; subway, 72

suicide, rates of: black vs. white, 3, 5, 5 *n.*, 134, 141; black vs. white homosexuals, 68; Japan, 133; rural vs. urban, 46, 132–133

Sweden, suicide in, 137–138, 141

Taylor, Gloria, case of, 116–120, 159, 161

Thematic Apperception Test, 15 *n.*, 20 *n.*, 24 *n.*, 27 *n.*, 33 *n.*, 36 *n.*, 78 *n.*, 79 *n.*, 82 *n.*, 103 *n.*, 107 *n.*, 112 *n.*, 119 *n.*, 127 *n.*; boy-violin card, 36 *n.*, 142, 161; discussion of, 156, 162; father-daughter card, 162; father-son card, 161–162; mother-son card, 15 *n.*
Tracy, Ina, case of, 22–24, 28, 29, 32, 159, 161
train, as suicide method, *see* subway

Uncle Toms, 140
United States, suicide in, 46
upward social mobility, 141

Vallen, Andrew, case of, 54–59, 66, 67, 161
violence, 9–16, 20, 20 *n.*, 21, 24–25, 27–31, 33, 35, 36, 38, 40, 41, 43–45, 56, 58, 69, 91–92, 103, 112 *n.*, 123, 124, 125, 127, 128, 139
visions, 35

Warner, Edward, case of, 85–90, 158, 161
Wayne, Jean, case of, 111–115, 120, 161
Wechsler Adult Intelligence Scale (WAIS), 12 *n.*, 16 *n.*, 40 *n.*; discussion of, 156, 157, 158
Weilen, Barbara, case of, 97–101, 120, 158, 161, 162
Weiner, Louis, viii
Williams, Glenda, case of, 39–41, 44
work experience, 15–21, 26, 30, 31, 33, 35, 39, 44, 50–51, 54, 58, 63, 72–74, 81, 85, 87, 94, 98, 99, 102, 105, 107, 109, 112–114, 118, 120, 126, 140–142

X, Malcolm, 125, 142

Zitrin, Arthur, viii